THE HOLY EARTH

THE
HOLY EARTH

By
L. H. BAILEY

MICHIGAN STATE UNIVERSITY PRESS
EAST LANSING

Michigan State University Press
East Lansing, Michigan 48823-5245

Printed and bound in the United States of America.

14 13 12 11 10 09 08   1 2 3 4 5 6 7 8 9 10

Original edition of *The Holy Earth* by L. H. Bailey was published in 1915
by C. Scribner's Sons, New York.

LIBRARY OF CONGRESS CATALOGING-IN-PUBLICATION DATA

Bailey, L. H. (Liberty Hyde), 1858–1954.
    The holy earth / by L. H. Bailey.
        p. cm.
    Originally published: New York : Christian Rural Fellowship, 1943.
    With new pref. and chronology.
    ISBN 978-0-87013-832-4 (pbk. : alk. paper)   1. Country life.
    2. Earth.   3. Natural resources.   I. Title.
    S521.B16   2008
    179'.1—dc22   2008024644

Cover design by Heather Truelove Aiston
Cover photograph by George Daniel is of the statue of Liberty Hyde
Bailey that stands in the Michigan State Horticultural Gardens. Used
with permission.

ℊ green Michigan State University Press is a member of the Green
press Press Initiative and is committed to developing and
INITIATIVE
encouraging ecologically responsible publishing practices. For more
information about the Green Press Initiative and the use of recycled
paper in book publishing, please visit *www.greenpressinitiative.org.*

Visit Michigan State University Press on the World Wide Web at:
www.msupress.msu.edu

Contents

Contents

Preface

In 1520, Robert Whittinton coined the phrase "a man for all seasons" to describe his friend, Thomas More. Whatever Whittinton's original intent, we have come to use the phrase to describe the rare polymath whose influence extends far beyond a parochial definition of vocation. Liberty Hyde Bailey's life perfectly straddles the transition from the nineteenth to the twentieth century, perhaps the last time when such a term might comfortably be applied. In innumerable ways, Bailey's life also mirrors the idealized expectations of the American experience—a person of humble and rural origin, who, by virtue of hard work and talent, rises to a position of prominence in the plant sciences, plant breeding, education, public administration and policy, public speaking, commerce, sociology, philosophy, and the arts. Bailey was a prodigious writer, authoring 63 books (including his 1,000 page monograph on raspberries), more than 100 scientific papers, and at least 1,300 articles on a wide variety of subjects. In addition, he edited more than 100 other books as well as numerous magazines.

Nestled among this considerable output is a seemingly modest collection of five titles, ranging from philosophy to poetry, variously known as the "Background Books" or the "Philosophy of the Holy Earth series." These books represent an extended discourse, interconnected across multiple dimensions, dealing with the overarching theme of humanity's place in the universe, with a common focus on our relationship with and responsibilities to the natural world. *The Holy Earth* is the first title in the series (1915) and is an extremely well-crafted argument that, despite a slightly dated style, pulls the reader inexorably toward a new perspective of environmental stewardship.

The title implies a religious basis for Bailey's polemic, but the reality is more nuanced. Contemporary discourse in the area of environmental policy is strongly influenced by the tension created by the claim of some environmentalists that our present problems are the result of a Judeo-Christian doctrine of environmental domination rather than constructive engagement. Bailey sidesteps many of the elements of the current debate and, in doing so, promotes a doctrine that is both transcendental and transforming. I find it doubtful that Bailey's discourse reflects a specific religious doctrine. Rather we see a Deist of strong spiritual sensitivity, struggling to redefine relationships that he feels have been corrupted by history.

Much of the discourse on the subject of human domination of nature involves images of conquest behaviors that pacify and subjugate nature for the sake of human good. Bailey rejects such notions out-of-hand. While nature may have a very wide scope, the earth—the abode of all life—cannot be anything but good:

> It is good to live. We talk of death and of lifelessness, but we know only of life. Even our prophecies of death are prophecies of more life. We know no better world: whatever else there may be is of things hoped for, not of things seen.

His second key proposition, embodied in the book's title, is the concept of the Earth as a holy system. In Bailey's view, this attribute of holiness arises directly out of the fact that the Earth, and everything that was initially in it, was the product of divine creation. Bailey does not dispute that idea that humans have dominion over the planet, but proposes that the confluence of holiness and dominion generate a new mandate:

> If the earth is holy, then the things that grow out of the earth are also holy. They do not belong to man to do with them as he will. There are many generations of folk yet to come after us, who will have equal right with us to the products of the globe.

In Bailey's view, righteous use—what others might call righteous stewardship—demands a new formulation of the relationship between humans and nature and that the nature of that reformulation rests solidly on moral propositions.

Bailey was a thorough-going Darwinian, and he knew that the world of life has been changing from the beginning. The advent of humans, their subsequent proliferation, and their mastery of science and technology combined to increase the potential for change. If numbers and technology were unbridled by moral imperatives, he saw a future of increasing degradation of humanity's birthright. Contemporary environmental debate tends to take two approaches to persuasion, both of which are evident in polemics such as Al Gore's *Inconvenient Truth*. The first is an appeal to numbers—science of the case—while the second is an appeal to self interest, be it our own or that of our grandchildren. Bailey avoids both of these arguments. He feels no need to appeal to science when the degradation of the environment should be plainly visible to anyone who looks at the issue with an unbiased eye. He also avoids a direct appeal to self interest, for he appears to feel that self interest is a key element in the historical evolution of the current crisis.

We live a technologically more sophisticated world than that of Bailey and, given the issues, an appeal to moral precepts and a new, spiritually based environmental ethic may seem naïve. This view is almost certainly short sighted. The majority of the humans with whom we share this fragile planet consider spirituality, in a myriad of forms, to be an essential part of their worldview. Much of what Bailey proposes has the potential to resonate with large numbers of people who are not part of the scientific mainstream. As such, this reprint of Bailey's seminal environmental work is not simply a matter of bringing a 90-year-old book back into the marketplace. Instead, it opens the mind of a true "man for all seasons" and hopefully can contribute to a long-delayed consensus regarding our place in nature.

RALPH E. TAGGART
Professor of Plant Biology
Michigan State University

1858-1954

Retrospect for the 1943 Edition by L. H. Bailey

MANY YEARS have passed since *The Holy Earth* was written. I think I have not read the book since the proofs left my hands nearly thirty years ago. Others have read it in more recent time, and I have agreed to their request for a reprint.

The book was my expression of an experience in life. I was born against the primeval forest. My youth was on the farm cut from that forest. I grew up with woodsmen and settlers and pioneers. Indians still inhabited the region. Wild animals were numerous. Passenger pigeons had a vast colony. It was a rigorous and wholesome discipline. Then I taught with and for country folk. All these experiences were against the background of simple and natural conditions.

I had been impressed with the fact that nature repairs and reconstructs itself. It provides its own healing. If the farm is wholly abandoned, nature takes it over and in time rears a new forest and builds new land. The city and the factory do not rebuild themselves when neglected or abandoned: they, too, in the processes of time return to forest or desert or plain. The circumstances of the native earth are the essential background of the race of men. What should be the spiritual and emotional reaction of the race of men to these circumstances? The book attempted to express an attitude.

The Holy Earth was written mostly on ship in the South Seas. I had been impressed again on long journeys with the majesty and fertility of the waters. I was not thinking of land alone. The sea is the larger part of the earth. I had in mind the planet on which men live. The planet is part of a program we do not comprehend but in which we may partake. We manipulate the surface of the earth for good or for ill. We must keep and protect the heritage for the millions who are to come after us. This is a moral obligation.

We did not make the earth. We have received it and its bounties. If it is beyond us, so is it divine. We have inescapable responsibilities. It is our privilege so to comprehend the use of the earth as to develop a spiritual stature. When the epoch of mere exploitation of the earth shall have worn itself out, we shall realize the heritage that remains and enter new realms of satisfaction.

THE HOLY EARTH

THE HOLY EARTH

First, the Statement

SO BOUNTIFUL hath been the earth and so securely have we drawn from it our substance, that we have taken it all for granted as if it were only a gift, and with little care or conscious thought of the consequences of our use of it; nor have we very much considered the essential relation that we bear to it as living parts in the vast creation. *righteousness*

It is good to think of ourselves—of this teeming, tense, and aspiring human race—as a helpful and contributing part in the plan of a cosmos, and as participators in some far-reaching destiny. The idea of responsibility is much asserted of late, but we relate it mostly to the attitude of persons in the realm of conventional conduct, which we have come to regard as very exclusively the realm of morals; and we have established certain formalities that satisfy the conscience. But there is some deeper relation than all this, which we must recognize and the consequences of which we must practise. There is a directer and more personal obligation than that which expends itself in loyalty to the manifold organizations and social requirements of the present day. There is a more fundamental co-operation in the scheme of things than that which deals with the proprieties or which centres about the selfishness too often expressed in the salvation of one's soul.

We can be only onlookers on that part of the cosmos that we call the far heavens, but it is possible to co-operate in the processes on the surface of the sphere. This co-operation may be conscious and definite, and also useful to the earth; that is, it may be real. What means this contact with our natural situation, this relationship to the earth to which we are born, and what signify this new exploration and conquest of the planet and these accumulating prophecies of science? Does the mothership of the earth have any real meaning to us?

All this does not imply a relation only with material and physical things, nor any effort to substitute a nature religion. Our relation with the planet must be raised into the realm of spirit; we cannot be fully useful otherwise. We must find a way to maintain the emotions in the abounding commercial civilization. There are two kinds of materials,—those of the native earth and the idols of one's hands. The latter are much in evidence in modern life, with the conquests of engineering, mechanics, architecture, and all the rest. We visualize them everywhere, and particularly in the great centres of population. The tendency is to be removed farther and farther from the everlasting backgrounds. Our religion is detached.

We come out of the earth and we have a right to the use of the materials; and there is no danger of crass materialism if we recognize the original materials as divine and if we understand our proper relation to the creation, for then will gross selfishness in the use of them be removed. This will necessarily mean a better conception of property and of one's obligation in the use of it. We shall conceive of the earth, which is the common habitation, as inviolable. One does not act rightly toward one's fellows if one does not know how to act rightly toward the earth.

Nor does this close regard for the mother earth imply any loss of mysticism or of exaltation: quite the contrary. Science but increases the mystery of the unknown and enlarges the boundaries of the spiritual vision. To feel that one is a useful and co-operating part in nature is to give one kinship, and to open the mind to the great resources and the high enthusiasms. Here arise the fundamental common relations. Here arise also the great emotions and conceptions of sublimity and

The right relationship named

grandeur, of majesty and awe, the uplift of vast desires,—
when one contemplates the earth and the universe and desires
to take them into the soul and to express oneself in their
terms; and here also the responsible practices of life take root.

So much are we now involved in problems of human groups,
so persistent are the portrayals of our social afflictions, and
so well do we magnify our woes by insisting on them, so
much in sheer weariness do we provide antidotes to soothe our
feelings and to cause us to forget by means of many empty
diversions, that we may neglect to express ourselves in simple
free personal joy and to separate the obligation of the individual from the irresponsibilities of the mass.

In the beginning

It suits my purpose to quote the first sentence in the Hebrew Scripture: In the beginning God created the heaven and the earth.

This is a statement of tremendous reach, introducing the cosmos; for it sets forth in the fewest words the elemental fact that the formation of the created earth lies above and before man, and that therefore it is not man's but God's. Man finds himself upon it, with many other creatures, all parts in some system which, since it is beyond man and superior to him, is divine.

Yet the planet was not at once complete when life had appeared upon it. The whirling earth goes through many vicissitudes; the conditions on its fruitful surface are ever-changing; and the forms of life must meet the new conditions: so does the creation continue, and every day sees the genesis in process. All life contends, sometimes ferociously but more often bloodlessly and benignly, and the contention results in momentary equilibrium, one set of contestants balancing another; but every change in the outward conditions destroys the equation and a new status results. Of all the disturbing living factors, man is the greatest. He sets mighty changes going, destroying forests, upturning the sleeping prairies, flooding the deserts, deflecting the courses of the rivers, building great cities. He operates consciously and increasingly with plan aforethought; and therefore he carries heavy responsibility.

This responsibility is recognized in the Hebrew Scripture, from which I have quoted; and I quote it again because I know of no other Scripture that states it so well. Man is given the image of the creator, even when formed from the dust of

4

the earth, so complete is his power and so real his dominion: And God blessed them: and God said unto them, Be fruitful, and multiply, and replenish the earth, and subdue it; and have dominion over the fish of the sea, and over the fowl of the air, and over every living thing that moveth upon the earth.

One cannot receive all these privileges without bearing the obligation to react and to partake, to keep, to cherish, and to co-operate. We have assumed that there is no obligation to an inanimate thing, as we consider the earth to be: but man should respect the conditions in which he is placed; the earth yields the living creature; man is a living creature; science constantly narrows the gulf between the animate and the in-animate, between the organized and the inorganized; evolution derives the creatures from the earth; the creation is one creation. I must accept all or reject all.

The earth is good

It is good to live. We talk of death and of lifelessness, but we know only of life. Even our prophecies of death are prophecies of more life. We know no better world: whatever else there may be is of things hoped for, not of things seen. The objects are here, not hidden nor far to seek: And God saw everything that he had made, and, behold, it was very good.

These good things are the present things and the living things. The account is silent on the things that were not created, the chaos, the darkness, the abyss. Plato, in the "Republic," reasoned that the works of the creator must be good because the creator is good. This goodness is in the essence of things; and we sadly need to make it a part in our philosophy of life. The earth is the scene of our life, and probably the very source of it. The heaven, so far as human beings know, is the source only of death; in fact, we have peopled it with the dead. We have built our philosophy on the dead.

We seem to have overlooked the goodness of the earth in the establishing of our affairs, and even in our philosophies. It is reserved as a theme for preachers and for poets. And yet, the goodness of the planet is the basic fact in our existence.

I am not speaking of good in an abstract way, in the sense in which some of us suppose the creator to have expressed himself as pleased or satisfied with his work. The earth is good in itself, and its products are good in themselves. The earth sustains all things. It satisfies. It matters not whether this satisfaction is the result of adaptation in the process of evolution; the fact remains that the creation is good.

To the common man the earth propounds no system of philosophy or of theology. The man makes his own personal contact, deals with the facts as they are or as he conceives

6

belief

them to be, and is not swept into any system. He has no right to assume a bad or evil earth, although it is difficult to cast off the hindrance of centuries of teaching. When he is properly educated he will get a new resource from his relationships.

It may be difficult to demonstrate this goodness. In the nature of things we must assume it, although we know that we could not subsist on a sphere of the opposite qualities. The important consideration is that we appreciate it, and this not in any sentimental and impersonal way. To every bird the air is good; and a man knows it is good if he is worth being a man. To every fish the water is good. To every beast its food is good, and its time of sleep is good. The creatures experience that life is good. Every man in his heart knows that there is goodness and wholeness in the rain, in the wind, the soil, the sea, the glory of sunrise, in the trees, and in the sustenance that we derive from the planet. When we grasp the significance of this situation, we shall forever supplant the religion of fear with a religion of consent.

We are so accustomed to these essentials—to the rain, the wind, the soil, the sea, the sunrise, the trees, the sustenance— that we may not include them in the categories of the good things, and we endeavor to satisfy ourselves with many small and trivial and exotic gratifications; and when these gratifications fail or pall, we find ourselves helpless and resourceless. The joy of sound sleep, the relish of a sufficient meal of plain and wholesome food, the desire to do a good day's work and the recompense when at night we are tired from the doing of it, the exhilaration of fresh air, the exercise of the natural powers, the mastery of a situation or a problem,— these and many others like them are fundamental satisfactions, beyond all pampering and all toys, and they are of the essence of goodness. I think we should teach all children how good are the common necessities, and how very good are the things that are made in the beginning.

It is kindly

We hear much about man being at the mercy of nature, and the literalist will contend that there can be no holy relation under such conditions. But so is man at the mercy of God.

It is a blasphemous practice that speaks of the hostility of the earth, as if the earth were full of menaces and cataclysms. The old fear of nature, that peopled the earth and sky with imps and demons, and that gave a future state to Satan, yet possesses the minds of men, only that we may have ceased to personify and to demonize our fears, although we still persistently contrast what we call the evil and the good. Still do we attempt to propitiate and appease the adversaries. Still do we carry the ban of the early philosophy that assumed materials and "the flesh" to be evil, and that found a way of escape only in renunciation and asceticism.

Nature cannot be antagonistic to man, seeing that man is a product of nature. We should find vast joy in the fellowship, something like the joy of Pan. We should feel the relief when we no longer apologize for the creator because of the things that are made.

It is true that there are devastations of flood and fire and frost, scourge of disease, and appalling convulsions of earthquake and eruption. But man prospers; and we know that the catastrophes are greatly fewer than the accepted bounties. We have no choice but to abide. No growth comes from hostility. It would undoubtedly be a poor human race if all the pathway had been plain and easy.

The contest with nature is wholesome, particularly when pursued in sympathy and for mastery. It is worthy a being created in God's image. The earth is perhaps a stern earth, but it is a kindly earth.

8

The human task:
to contend (p 4)
+ to abide

It Is Kindly

Most of our difficulty with the earth lies in the effort to do what perhaps ought not to be done. Not even all the land is fit to be farmed. A good part of agriculture is to learn how to adapt one's work to nature, to fit the crop-scheme to the climate and to the soil and the facilities. To live in right relation with his natural conditions is one of the first lessons that a wise farmer or any other wise man learns. We are at pains to stress the importance of conduct; very well: conduct toward the earth is an essential part of it.

Nor need we be afraid of any fact that makes one fact more or less in the sum of contacts between the earth and the earth-born children. All "higher criticism" adds to the faith rather than subtracts from it, and strengthens the bond between. The earth and its products are very real.

Our outlook has been drawn very largely from the abstract. Not being yet prepared to understand the conditions of nature, man considered the earth to be inhospitable, and he looked to the supernatural for relief; and relief was heaven. Our pictures of heaven are of the opposites of daily experience,—of release, of peace, of joy uninterrupted. The hunting-grounds are happy and the satisfaction has no end. The habit of thought has been set by this conception, and it colors our dealings with the human questions and to much extent it controls our practice.

But we begin to understand that the best dealing with problems on earth is to found it on the facts of earth. This is the contribution of natural science, however abstract, to human welfare. Heaven is to be a real consequence of life on earth; and we do not lessen the hope of heaven by increasing our affection for the earth, but rather do we strengthen it. Men now forget the old images of heaven, that they are mere sojourners and wanderers lingering for deliverance, pilgrims in a strange land. Waiting for this rescue, with posture and formula and phrase, we have overlooked the essential good-ness and quickness of the earth and the immanence of God.

This feeling that we are pilgrims in a vale of tears has been

9

enhanced by the wide-spread belief in the sudden ending of the world, by collision or some other impending disaster, and in the common apprehension of doom; and lately by speculations as to the aridation and death of the planet, to which all of us have given more or less credence. But most of these notions are now considered to be fantastic, and we are increasingly confident that the earth is not growing old in a human sense, that its atmosphere and its water are held by the attraction of its mass, and that the sphere is at all events so permanent as to make little difference in our philosophy and no difference in our good behavior.

I am again impressed with the first record in Genesis in which some mighty prophet-poet began his account with the creation of the physical universe.

So do we forget the old-time importance given to mere personal salvation, which was permission to live in heaven, and we think more of our present situation, which is the situation of obligation and of service; and he who loses his life shall save it.

We begin to foresee the vast religion of a better social order.

The earth is holy

Verily, then, the earth is divine, because man did not make it. We are here, part in the creation. We cannot escape. We are under obligation to take part and to do our best, living with each other and with all the creatures. We may not know the full plan, but that does not alter the relation. When once we set ourselves to the pleasure of our dominion, reverently and hopefully, and assume all its responsibilities, we shall have a new hold on life.

We shall put our dominion into the realm of morals. It is now in the realm of trade. This will be very personal morals, but it will also be national and racial morals. More iniquity follows the improper and greedy division of the resources and privileges of the earth than any other form of sinfulness.

If God created the earth, so is the earth hallowed; and if it is hallowed, so must we deal with it devotedly and with care that we do not despoil it, and mindful of our relations to all beings that live on it. We are to consider it religiously: Put off thy shoes from off thy feet, for the place whereon thou standest is holy ground.

The sacredness to us of the earth is intrinsic and inherent. It lies in our necessary relationship and in the duty imposed upon us to have dominion, and to exercise ourselves even against our own interests. We may not waste that which is not ours. To live in sincere relations with the company of created things and with conscious regard for the support of all men now and yet to come, must be of the essence of righteousness.

This is a larger and more original relation than the modern attitude of appreciation and admiration of nature. In the days of the patriarchs and prophets, nature and man shared in the condemnation and likewise in the redemption. The ground was cursed for Adam's sin. Paul wrote that the whole creation groaneth and travaileth in pain, and that it waiteth for the revealing. Isaiah proclaimed the redemption of the wilderness and the solitary place with the redemption of man, when they shall rejoice and blossom as the rose, and when the glowing sand shall become a pool and the thirsty ground springs of water.

The usual objects have their moral significance. An oak-tree is to us a moral object because it lives its life regularly and fulfils its destiny. In the wind and in the stars, in forest and by the shore, there is spiritual refreshment: And the spirit of God moved upon the face of the waters.

I do not mean all this, for our modern world, in any vague or abstract way. If the earth is holy, then the things that grow out of the earth are also holy. They do not belong to man to do with them as he will. Dominion does not carry personal ownership. There are many generations of folk yet to come after us, who will have equal right with us to the products of the globe. It would seem that a divine obligation rests on every soul. Are we to make righteous use of the vast accumulation of knowledge of the planet? If so, we must have a new formulation. The partition of the earth among the millions who live on it is necessarily a question of morals; and a society that is founded on an unmoral partition and use cannot itself be righteous and whole.

Second, the Consequences

I HAVE now stated my purpose; and the remainder of the little book will make some simple applications of it and draw some inferences therefrom. There is nothing here that need alarm the timid, albeit we enter a disputed field, a field of opinion rather than of demonstration; and if the reader goes with me, I trust that we may have a pleasant journey.

It is to be a journey of recognition, not of protest. It is needful that we do not forget.

We are not to enter into a course of reasoning with those whom we meet on the way, or to pause to debate the definitions and analyses made in books, or to deny any of the satisfactions of tradition. We shall be ready for impressions; and possibly we shall be able to find some of the old truths in unfrequented places.

The habit of destruction

The first observation that must be apparent to all men is that our dominion has been mostly destructive.

We have been greatly engaged in digging up the stored resources, and in destroying vast products of the earth for some small kernel that we can apply to our necessities or add to our enjoyments. We excavate the best of the coal and cast away the remainder; blast the minerals and metals from underneath the crust, and leave the earth raw and sore; we box the pines for turpentine and abandon the growths of limitless years to fire and devastation; sweep the forests with the besom of destruction; pull the fish from the rivers and ponds without making any adequate provision for renewal; exterminate whole races of animals; choke the streams with refuse and dross; rob the land of its available stores, denuding the surface, exposing great areas to erosion.

Nor do we exercise the care and thrift of good housekeepers. We do not clean up our work or leave the earth in order. The remnants and accumulation of mining-camps are left to ruin and decay; the deserted phosphate excavations are ragged, barren, and unfilled; vast areas of forested lands are left in brush and waste, unthoughtful of the future, unmindful of the years that must be consumed to reduce the refuse to mould and to cover the surface respectably, uncharitable to those who must clear away the wastes and put the place in order; and so thoughtless are we with these natural resources that even the establishments that manufacture them—the mills, the factories of many kinds—are likely to be offensive objects in the landscape, unclean, unkempt, displaying the unconcern of the owners to the obligation that the use of the materials imposes and to the sensibilities of the com-

The Habit of Destruction

munity for the way in which they handle them. The burden of proof seems always to have been rested on those who partake little in the benefits, although we know that these nonpartakers have been real owners of the resources; and yet so undeveloped has been the public conscience in these matters that the blame—if blame there be—cannot be laid on one group more than on the other. Strange it is, however, that we should not have insisted at least that those who appropriate the accumulations of the earth should complete their work, cleaning up the remainders, leaving the areas wholesome, inoffensive, and safe. How many and many are the years required to grow a forest and to fill the pockets of the rocks, and how satisfying are the landscapes, and yet how desperately soon may men reduce it all to ruin and to emptiness, and how slatternly may they violate the scenery!

All this habit of destructiveness is uneconomic in the best sense, unsocial, unmoral.

Society now begins to demand a constructive process. With care and with regard for other men, we must produce the food and the other supplies in regularity and sufficiency; and we must clean up after our work, that the earth may not be depleted, scarred, or repulsive.

Yet there is even a more defenseless devastation than all this. It is the organized destructiveness of those who would make military domination the major premise in the constitution of society, accompanying desolation with viciousness and violence, ravaging the holy earth, disrespecting the works of the creator, looking toward extirpation, confessing thereby that they do not know how to live in cooperation with their fellows; in such situations, every new implement of destruction adds to the guilt.

In times past we were moved by religious fanaticism, even to the point of waging wars. Today we are moved by impulses of trade, and we find ourselves plunged into a war of commercial frenzy; and as it has behind it vaster resources and more command of natural forces, so is it the most ferocious and wasteful that the race has experienced, exceeding in its havoc the cataclysms of earthquake and volcano. Certainly we have not yet learned how to withstand the prosperity and the privileges that we have gained by the discoveries of science; and certainly the morals of commerce has not given us freedom or mastery. Rivalry that leads to arms is a natural fruit of unrestrained rivalry in trade.

Man has dominion, but he has no commission to devastate: And the Lord God took the man, and put him into the garden of Eden to dress it and to keep it.

Verily, so bountiful hath been the earth and so securely have we drawn from it our substance, that we have taken it all for granted as if it were only a gift, and with little care or conscious thought of the consequences of our use of it.

The new hold

We may distinguish three stages in our relation to the planet,—the collecting stage, the mining stage, and the producing stage. These overlap and perhaps are nowhere distinct, and yet it serves a purpose to contrast them.

At first man sweeps the earth to see what he may gather,— game, wood, fruits, fish, fur, feathers, shells on the shore. A certain social and moral life arises out of this relation, seen well in the woodsmen and the fishers—in whom it best persists to the present day—strong, dogmatic, superstitious folk. Then man begins to go beneath the surface to see what he can find,—iron and precious stones, the gold of Ophir, coal, and many curious treasures. This develops the exploiting faculties, and leads men into the uttermost parts. In both these stages the elements of waste and disregard have been heavy.

Finally, we begin to enter the productive stage, whereby we secure supplies by controlling the conditions under which they grow, wasting little, harming not. Farming has been very much a mining process, the utilizing of fertility easily at hand and the moving-on to lands unspoiled of quick potash and nitrogen. Now it begins to be really productive and constructive, with a range of responsible and permanent morals. We rear the domestic animals with precision. We raise crops, when we will, almost to a nicety. We plant fish in lakes and streams to some extent but chiefly to provide more game rather than more human food, for in this range we are yet mostly in the collecting or hunter stage. If the older stages were strongly expressed in the character of the people, so will this new stage be expressed; and so is it that we are escaping the primitive and should be coming into a new character. We shall find our rootage in the soil.

The Holy Earth

This new character, this clearer sense of relationship with the earth, should express itself in all the people and not exclusively in farming people and their like. It should be a popular character—or a national character if we would limit the discussion to one people—and not a class character. Now, here lies a difficulty and here is a reason for writing this book: the population of the earth is increasing, the relative population of farmers is decreasing, people are herding in cities, we have a city mind, and relatively fewer people are brought into touch with the earth in any real way. So is it incumbent on us to take special pains—now that we see the new time—that all the people, or as many of them as possible, shall have contact with the earth and that the earth righteousness shall be abundantly taught.

I hasten to say that I am not thinking of any back-to-the-farm movement to bring about the results we seek. Necessarily, the proportion of farmers will decrease. Not so many are needed, relatively, to produce the requisite supplies from the earth. Agriculture makes a great contribution to human progress by releasing men for the manufactures and the trades. In proportion as the ratio of farmers decreases is it important that we provide them the best of opportunities and encouragement: they must be better and better men. And if we are to secure our moral connection with the planet to a large extent through them, we can see that they bear a relation to society in general that we have overlooked.

Even the farming itself is changing radically in character. It ceases to be an occupation to gain sustenance and becomes a business. We apply to it the general attitudes of commerce. We must be alert to see that it does not lose its capacity for spiritual contact.

How we may achieve a more wide-spread contact with the earth on the part of all the people without making them farmers, I shall endeavor to suggest as I proceed; in fact, this is my theme. Dominion means mastery; we may make the surface of the earth much what we will; we can govern the way in which we shall contemplate it. We are probably near something like a stable occupancy. It is not to be expected that there will be vast shifting of cities as the contest for the mastery of the earth proceeds,—probably nothing like the loss of Tyre and Carthage, and of the commercial glory of Venice. In fact, we shall have a progressive occupancy. The greater the population, the greater will be the demands on the planet; and, moreover, every new man will make more demands than his father made, for he will want more to satisfy him. We are to take from the earth much more than we have ever taken before, but it will be taken in a new way and with better intentions. It will be seen, therefore, that we are not here dealing narrowly with an occupation but with something very fundamental to our life on the planet.

We are not to look for our permanent civilization to rest on any species of robber-economy. No flurry of coal-mining, or gold-fever, or rubber-collecting in the tropics, or excitement of prospecting for new finds or even locating new lands, no ravishing of the earth or monopolistic control of its bounties, will build a stable society. So is much of our economic and social fabric transitory. It is not by accident that a very distinct form of society is developing in the great farming regions of the Mississippi Valley and in other comparable places; the exploiting and promoting occupancy of those lands is passing and a stable progressive development appears. We have been obsessed of the passion to cover everything at once, to skin the earth, to pass on, even when there was no necessity for so doing. It is a vast pity that this should ever have been the policy of government in giving away great tracts of land by lottery, as if our fingers would burn if we held the lands inviolate until needed by the natural process of settlement. The people should be kept on their lands long enough to learn how to use them. But very well: we have run with the wind, we have staked the lands; now we shall be real farmers and real conquerors. Not all lands are equally good for farming, and some lands will never be good for farming; but whether in Iowa, or New England, or old Asia, farming land may develop character in the people.

My reader must not infer that we have arrived at a permanent agriculture, although we begin now to see the importance of a permanent land occupancy. Probably we have not yet evolved a satisfying husbandry that will maintain itself century by century, without loss and without the ransacking of the ends of the earth for fertilizer materials to make good our deficiencies. All the more is it important that the problem be elevated into the realm of statesmanship and of morals. Neither must he infer that the resources of the earth are to be locked up beyond contact and use (for the contact and use will be morally regulated). But no system of brilliant exploitation, and no accidental scratching of the surface of the earth, and no easy appropriation of stored materials can suffice us in the good days to come. City, country, this class and that class, all fall and merge before the common necessity.

It is often said that the farmer is our financial mainstay; so in the good process of time will he be a moral mainstay, for ultimately finance and social morals must coincide.

The gifts are to be used for service and for satisfaction, and not for wealth. Very great wealth introduces too many intermediaries, too great indirectness, too much that is extrinsic, too frequent hindrances and superficialities. It builds a wall about the man, and too often does he receive his impressions of the needs of the world from satellites and sycophants. It is significant that great wealth, if it contributes much to social service, usually accomplishes the result by endowing others to work. The gift of the products of the earth was "for meat": nothing was said about riches.

Yet the very appropriation or use of natural resources may be the means of directing the mind of the people back to the native situations. We have the opportunity to make the forthcoming development of water-power, for example, such an agency for wholesome training. Whenever we can appropriate without despoliation or loss, or without a damaging monopoly, we tie the people to the backgrounds.

In the background is the countryman; and how is the countryman to make use of the rain and the abounding soil, and the varied wonder of plant and animal amidst which he lives, that he may arrive at kinship? We are teaching him how to bring some of these things under the dominion of his hands, how to measure and to weigh and to judge. This will give him the essential physical mastery. But beyond this, how shall he take them into himself, how shall he make them to be of his spirit, how shall he complete his dominion? How shall he become the man that his natural position requires of him? This will come slowly, ah, yes!—slowly. The people—the great striving self-absorbed throng of the people—they do not know what we mean when we talk like this, they hear only so many fine words. The naturist knows that the time will come slowly, —not yet are we ready for fulfilment; he knows that we cannot regulate the cosmos, or even the natural history of the people, by enactments. Slowly: by removing handicaps here and there; by selection of the folk in a natural process, to eliminate the unresponsive; by teaching, by suggestion; by a public recognition of the problem, even though not one of us sees the end of it.

I hope my reader now sees where I am leading him. He sees that I am not thinking merely of instructing the young in the names and habits of birds and flowers and other pleasant knowledge, although this works strongly toward the desired end; nor of any movement merely to have gardens, or to own farms, although this is desirable provided one is qualified to own a farm; nor of rhapsodies on the beauties of nature. Nor am I thinking of any new plan or any novel kind of institution or any new agency; rather shall we do better to escape some of the excessive institutionalism and organization. We are so accustomed to think in terms of organized politics and education and religion and philanthropies that when we detach ourselves we are said to lack definiteness. It is the personal satisfaction in the earth to which we are born, and the quickened responsibility, the whole relation, broadly developed, of the man and of all men,—it is this attitude that we are to discuss.

The years pass and they grow into centuries. We see more clearly. We are to take a new hold.

The brotherhood relation

A constructive and careful handling of the resources of the earth is impossible except on a basis of large co-operation and of association for mutual welfare. The great inventions and discoveries of recent time have extensive social significance.

Yet we have other relations than with the physical and static materials. We are parts in a living sensitive creation. The theme of evolution has overturned our attitude toward this creation. The living creation is not exclusively man-centred: it is bio-centric. We perceive the essential continuity in nature, arising from within rather than from without, the forms of life proceeding upwardly and onwardly in something very like a mighty plan of sequence, man being one part in the process. We have genetic relation with all living things, and our aristocracy is the aristocracy of nature. We can claim no gross superiority and no isolated self-importance. The creation, and not man, is the norm. Even now do we begin to guide our practises and our speech by our studies of what we still call the lower creation. We gain a good perspective on ourselves.

If we are parts in the evolution, and if the universe, or even the earth, is not made merely as a footstool, or as a theatre for man, so do we lose our cosmic selfishness and we find our place in the plan of things. We are emancipated from ignorance and superstition and small philosophies. The present wide-spread growth of the feeling of brotherhood would have been impossible in a self-centred creation: the way has been prepared by the discussion of evolution, which is the major biological contribution to human welfare and progress. This is the philosophy of the oneness in nature and the unity in living things.

The farmer's relation

The surface of the earth is particularly within the care of the farmer. He keeps it for his own sustenance and gain, but his gain is also the gain of all the rest of us. At the best, he accumulates little to himself. The successful farmer is the one who produces more than he needs for his support; and the overplus he does not keep; and, moreover, his own needs are easily satisfied. It is of the utmost consequence that the man next the earth shall lead a fair and simple life; for in riotous living he might halt many good supplies that now go to his fellows.

It is a public duty so to train the farmer that he shall appreciate his guardianship. He is engaged in a quasi-public business. He really does not even own his land. He does not take his land with him, but only the personal development that he gains from it. He cannot annihilate his land, as another might destroy all his belongings. He is the agent or the representative of society to guard and to subdue the surface of the earth; and he is the agent of the divinity that made it. He must exercise his dominion with due regard to all these obligations. He is a trustee. The productiveness of the earth must increase from generation to generation: this also is his obligation. He must handle all his materials, remembering man and remembering God. A man cannot be a good farmer unless he is a religious man.

If the farmer is engaged in a quasi-public business, shall we undertake to regulate him? This relationship carries a vast significance to the social order, and it must color our attitude toward the man on the land. We are now in that epoch of social development when we desire to regulate by law everything that is regulatable and the other things besides. It is

24

recently proposed that the Congress shall pass a law regulating the cropping scheme of the farmer for the protection of soil fertility. This follows the precedent of the regulation, by enactment, of trusts and public utilities. It is fortunate that such a law cannot be passed, and could not be enforced if it were passed; but this and related proposals are crude expressions of the growing feeling that the farmer owes an obligation to society, and that this obligation must be enforced and the tiller of the soil be held to account.

We shall produce a much better and safer man when we make him self-controlling by developing his sense of responsibility than when we regulate him by exterior enactments.

In the realm of control of the farming occupation we shall invoke other than legal means, and perhaps these means will be suggestive for other situations. These means may be somewhat indefinite in the law-book sense, but they may attain to a better human result. We shall reach the question by surer ways than the crudities of legislation. We shall reach the man, in this field, rather than his business. We have begun it by accepting it as one part of our duty to the race to provide liberally at public expense for the special education of the man on the land. This is the reason, even if we have not formulated it to ourselves, why society is willing to go farther in the education of the farming people than in the popular education of other ranges of the people. This, of course, is the fundamental way; and if there are any governments that attempt to safeguard this range directly by laws rather than by education, then they have not arrived at a long view of the situation.

We invoke regulatory law for the control of the corporate activities; but we must not forget the other kinds of activities contributing to the making of society, nor attempt to apply to them the same methods of correction.

Into this secular and more or less technical education we are now to introduce the element of moral obligation, that the man may understand his peculiar contribution and responsibility to society; but this result cannot be attained until the farmer and every one of us recognize the holiness of the earth.

The farmer and every one of us: every citizen should be put right toward the planet, should be quicked to his relationship to his natural background. The whole body of public sentiment should be sympathetic with the man who works and administers the land for us; and this requires understanding. We have heard much about the "marginal man," but the first concern of society should be for the bottom man.

If this philosophy should really be translated into action, the farmer would nowhere be a peasant, forming merely a caste, and that a low one, among his fellows. He would be an independent co-operating citizen partaking fully of the fruits of his labor, enjoying the social rewards of his essential position, being sustained and protected by a body of responsive public opinion. The farmer cannot keep the earth for us without an enlightened and very active support from every other person, and without adequate safeguards from exploitation and from unessential commercial pressure.

This social support requires a ready response on the part of the farmer; and he must also be developed into his position by a kind of training that will make him quickly and naturally responsive to it. The social fascination of the town will always be greater than that of the open country. The movements are more rapid, more picturesque, have more color and more vivacity. It is not to be expected that we can overcome this fascination and safeguard the country boy and girl merely by introducing more showy or active enterprises into the open country. We must develop a new background for the country youth, establish new standards, and arouse a new point of view. The farmer will not need all the things that the city man thinks the farmer needs. We must stimulate his moral response, his appreciation of the worthiness of the things in which he lives, and increase his knowledge of all the objects and affairs amongst which he moves. The backbone of the rural question is at the bottom a moral problem.

The Farmer's Relation

We do not yet know whether the race can permanently endure urban life, or whether it must be constantly renewed from the vitalities in the rear. We know that the farms and the back spaces have been the mother of the race. We know that the exigencies and frugalities of life in these backgrounds beget men and women to be serious and steady and to know the value of every hour and of every coin that they earn; and whenever they are properly trained, these folk recognize the holiness of the earth.

For some years I have had the satisfaction to speak to rural folk in many places on the holy earth and to make some of the necessary applications. Everywhere I have met the heartiest assent from these people. Specially do they respond to the suggestion that if the earth is hallowed, so are the native products of the earth hallowed; and they like to have the mystery —which is the essential sentiment—of these things brought home to them with frequency. I will here let my reader have a letter that one of these persons wrote me, and I print it without change. On inquiry, the writer of it told me that he is a farmer, has never followed any other occupation, was brought up "in the woods," and has had practically no education. I did not ask him, but I judge from the narrative style that he has been a reader or a hearer of the Old Testament; and here is the letter:

As you say, too many people confound farming, with that sordid, selfish, money-getting game, called "business," whereas, the farmer's position is administrative, being in a way a dispenser of the "Mysteries of God," for they are mysteries. Every apple is a mystery, and every potato is a mystery, and every ear of corn is a mystery, and every pound of butter is a mystery, and when a "farmer" is not able to understand these things he is out of place.

The farmer uses the soil and the rains and the snows and the frosts and the winds and the sun; these are also the implements of the Almighty, the only tools He uses, and while you were talking that day, it brought to mind the recollection of an account I once read of an occurrence which took place in the vicinity of Carlsruhe, in Germany, about thirty years ago, and I want to tell you about it. An old man and his two sons, who were laborers on a large farm there, went out one morning to mow peas,

The Holy Earth

with scythes, as was the method in use at that time, and soon after they began work, they noticed a large active man coming along a pathway which bordered the field on one side, and when he came to where they were, he spoke to them, very pleasantly, and asked them some questions about their work and taking the scythe from the hands of the older man he mowed some with it and finally returned it and went his way. After a time when the owner of the farm came out to oversee the work they told him of the occurrence, and asked him if he could tell who the stranger might be, and he told them that he was Prince Bismarck, the Chancellor of the empire, who was staying at his country home at Carlsruhe, and was out for his morning walk, and they were astonished, and the old man was filled with a great pride, and he felt himself elevated above all his fellows, and he wouldn't have sold his scythe for half the money in Germany, and his descendants to this day boast of the fact that their father and Bismarck mowed with the same scythe. Now if it was sufficient to stimulate the pride of this old laborer, if it was sufficient to create for him a private aristocracy, if it was sufficient to convert that old rusty scythe into a priceless heirloom to be treasured up and transmitted from father to son, if it was sufficient for all these things that he had once held a momentarily unimportant association with the man of "blood and iron," how much more inconceivably and immeasurably high and exalted is the station of the farmer who is, in a measure, a fellow craftsman of the God of Nature, of the great First Cause of all things, and people don't know it. No wonder the boys leave the farm!

The underlying training of a people

This, then, is the landsman's obligation, and his joyful privilege. But it must not be supposed that he alone bears the responsibility to maintain the holiness of the divine earth. It is the obligation also of all of us, since every one is born to the earth and lives upon it, and since every one must react to it to the extent of his place and capabilities. This being so, then it is a primary need that we shall place at the use of the people a kind of education that shall quicken these attachments.

Certainly all means of education are useful, and every means should be developed to its best; and it is not to be expected that all the people shall pursue a single means: but to the nation and to the race a fundamental training must be provided.

We are now in the time of developing a technical education in agriculture, to the end that we may produce our land supplies. Already this education is assuming broad aspects, and we begin to see that it has very important bearing on public policies. It is a new form of exercise in natural science, —the old education in this great realm having become so specialized and departmentalized as to lose much of its value as a means of popular training.

It is a happy augury that in North America so many public men and administrators have taken the large view of education by means of agriculture, desiring, while training farmers of those who would be farmers, to make it a means of bringing the understanding of the people back to the land. The Americans are making a very remarkable contribution here, in a spirit of real statesmanship. In the long run, this procedure will produce a spirit in the people that will have far-reaching importance in the development of national character, and in a relation to the backgrounds of which very few of us yet have vision.

It will be fortunate if we can escape the formalizing and professionalizing of this education, that has cast such a blight on most of the older means of training the young, and if we can keep it democratic and free in spirit.

We shall need to do the same in all the subjects that lie at the foundations,—in all the other crafts; all these crafts are of the earth. They support the physical man and the social fabric, and make the conditions out of which all the highest achievements may come.

Every person in a democracy has a right to be educated by these means; and a people living in a democracy must of necessity understand the significance of such education. This education should result or function politically. It is not sufficient to train technically in the trades and crafts and arts to the end of securing greater economic efficiency,—this may be accomplished in a despotism and result in no self-action on the part of the people. Every democracy must reach far beyond what is commonly known as economic efficiency, and do everything it can to enable those in the backgrounds to maintain their standing and their pride and to partake in the making of political affairs.

The neighbor's access to the earth

When one really feels the response to the native earth, one feels also the obligation and the impulse to share it with the neighbor.

The earth is not selfish. It is open and free to all. It invites everywhere. The naturist is not selfish,—he shares all his joys and discoveries, even to the extent of publishing them. The farmer is not selfish with his occupation,—he freely aids every one or any one to engage in his occupation, even if that one becomes his competitor. But occupations that are some degrees removed from the earth may display selfishness; trade and, to a large extent, manufacture are selfish, and they lock themselves in. Even the exploiting of the resources of the earth may be selfish, in the taking of the timber and the coal, the water-powers and the minerals, for all this is likely to develop to a species of plunder. The naturist desires to protect the plants and the animals and the situations for those less fortunate and for those who come after. There are lumbermen and miners with the finest sense of obligation. There are other men who would take the last nugget and destroy the last bole.

We are to recognize the essential integrity of the farming occupation, when developed constructively, as contrasted with the vast system of improbity and dishonor that arises from depredation and from the taking of booty.

The best kind of community interest attaches to the proper use and partitioning of the earth, a communism that is dissociated from propaganda and programs. The freedom of the earth is not the freedom of license: there is always the thought of the others that are dependent on it. It is the freedom of utilization for needs and natural desires, without regard to one's place among one's fellows, or even to one's condition

31

of degradation or state of sinfulness. All men are the same when they come back to the meadows, to the hills, and to the deep woods: He maketh his sun to rise on the evil and the good, and sendeth rain on the just and the unjust.

The lesson of the growing abounding earth is of liberality for all, and never exploitation or very exclusive opportunities for the few. Even if the weaker anywhere perish in the contest for food, they are nevertheless given the opportunity to contest on terms equal to their abilities; and at all events, we come, in the human sphere, to the domination of sweet reason rather than to competition in sheer force. When, by means of reasonable education, this simple relation is understood by mankind and begins to express itself spontaneously, we shall find our voluminous complex of laws to regulate selfishness gradually disappearing and passing into the limbo.

It is now easy to understand the sinfulness of vast private estates that shut up expanses of the surface of the earth from the reach and enjoyment of others that are born similarly to the privileges of the planet. There is no warrant in nature for guarantee deeds to such estates. It is true, of course, that land-estates should not be equal, for capacities for use are not equal, and abilities and deserts are not equal. It is legitimate to reward those who otherwise render great service, and this reward may lie in unusual privileges. The present emoluments in the way of incomes bear little relation to service or even to merit.

We have not yet escaped the idea that vested rights—and particularly personal realty—are inviolable. Certainly these rights must be protected by law, otherwise there can be no stability and regularity in affairs; but there is no inalienable right in the ownership of the surface of the earth. Readjustments must come, and even now they are coming slowly, and here and there in the interest of the neighbor; and in the end there will be no private monopoly of public or natural resources.

The cure for these ills does not lie, however, in the owner-

The Neighbor's Access to the Earth

ship of all the land by "the government," at least not in our time and perhaps never. It is well for a person to have his own plot for his life-time, with the right to use it as he will so long as he does not offend, or does not despoil it for those who follow: it steadies him, and it identifies him with a definite program in life.

We usually speak as if all good results in the distribution of the natural bounty will ensue if "the government" or "the state" owns the resources; but government ownership of resources and direction of industries may not mean freedom or escape for the people. It depends entirely on the kind of government,—not on its name or description, but on the extent to which the people have been trained to partake on their own initiative. The government may be an autocracy or only another form of monopoly.

The aristocracy of land has much to its credit. Great gains in human accomplishment have come out of it; but this does not justify it for the future. The aristocracy of land is a very dangerous power in human affairs. It is all the more dangerous when associated with aristocracy of birth and of factitious social position, which usually accompany it. A people may be ever so free in its advantages and in its theoretical political organization, and yet suffer overwhelming bondage if its land is tied up in an aristocratic system, and particularly if that system is connected into a social aristocracy. And whenever rigid aristocracy in land connects itself with the close control of politics, the subjection becomes final and complete.

What lies within a nation or a people may lie in enlarged form between the nations or the peoples. Neighborliness is international. Contest for land and sea is at the basis of wars. Recognizing the right of any people to its own life, we must equally recognize its right to a sufficient part of the surface of the earth. We must learn how to subdivide it on the basis of neighborliness, friendship, and conference; if we cannot learn this, then we cannot be neighbors but only enemies. The proposal now before Congress to cede to Canada the

Alaskan Panhandle, or a part of it, is an evidence of this growth of international morals, extended to the very basis on which nations have been the least ready to co-operate.

If we may fraternalize territory, so shall we fraternalize commerce. No people may rightly be denied the privilege to trade with all other peoples. All kinds of useful interchange are civilizers and peacemakers; and if we carry ourselves to others when we carry our produce and our wares, so do any of us need that others shall bring their produce and their wares to us. It would be a sorry people that purchased no supplies from without. Every people, small or large, has right of access to the sea, for the sea belongs to mankind. It follows that no people has a right to deprive any other people of the shore, if that people desires the contact.

We now begin to understand the awful sin of partitioning the earth by force.

The subdividing of the land

The question then arises whether lands and other natural resources shall now be divided and redistributed in order that the share-and-share of the earth's patrimony shall be morally just. Undoubtedly the logic of the situation makes for many personal points of very close contact with the mother earth, and contact is usually most definite and best when it results from what we understand as ownership. This, in practice, suggests many small parcels of land—for those who would have their contact by means of land, which is the directest means—under personal fee. But due provision must always be made, as I have already indicated, for the man who makes unusual contribution to the welfare of his fellows, that he may be allowed to extend his service and attain his own full development; and moreover, an established order may not be overturned suddenly and completely without much damage, not only to personal interests but to society. Every person should have the right and the privilege to a personal use of some part of the earth; and naturally the extent of his privilege must be determined by his use of it.

It is urged that lands can be most economically administered in very large units and under corporate management; but the economic results are not the most important results to be secured, although at present they are the most stressed. The ultimate good in the use of land is the development of the people; it may be better that more persons have contact with it than that it shall be executively more effectively administered. The morals of land management is more important than the economics of land management; and of course my reader is aware that by morals I mean the results that arise from a right use of the earth rather than the formal attitudes toward standardized or conventional codes of conduct.

If the moral and the economic ends can be secured simultaneously, as eventually they will be secured, the perfect results will come to pass; but any line of development founded on accountant economics alone will fail.

Here I must pause for an explanation in self-defense, for my reader may think I advise the "little farm well tilled" that has so much captured the public mind. So far from giving such advice, I am not thinking exclusively of farming when I speak of the partitioning of the land. One may have land merely to live on. Another may have a wood to wander in. One may have a spot on which to make a garden. Another may have a shore, and another a retreat in the mountains or in some far space. Much of the earth can never be farmed or mined or used for timber, and yet these supposed waste places may be very real assets to the race: we shall learn this in time. I am glad to see these outlying places set aside as public reserves; and yet we must not so organize and tie up the far spaces as to prevent persons of little means from securing small parcels. These persons should have land that they can handle and manipulate, in which they may dig, on which they may plant trees and build cabins, and which they may feel is theirs to keep and to master, and which they are not obliged to "improve." In the parks and reserves the land may be available only to look at, or as a retreat in which one may secure permission to camp. The regulations are necessary for these places, but these places are not sufficient.

If it were possible for every person to own a tree and to care for it, the good results would be beyond estimation.

Now, farming is a means of support; and in this case, the economic possibilities of a particular piece of land are of primary consequence. Of course, the most complete permanent contact with the earth is by means of farming, when one makes a living from the land; this should produce better results than hunting or sport; but one must learn how to make

The Subdividing of the Land

this connection. It is possible to hoe potatoes and to hear the birds sing at the same time, although our teaching has not much developed this completeness in the minds of the people.

I hope, therefore, that the farmer's piece of land will be economically good (that it may make him a living and produce a surplus for some of the rest of us), and that the farmer may be responsive to his situation. The size of the farm that is to support a family, and the kinds of crops that shall be grown and even the yields that shall be secured to the acre, are technical problems of agriculture. In this New World, with expensive labor and still with cheap land, we cannot yet afford to produce the high yields of some of the Old World places,—it may be better to till more land with less yield to the acre. But all this is aside from my present purpose; and this purpose is to suggest the very real importance of making it possible for an increasing proportion of the people to have close touch with the earth in their own rights and in their own names.

We recognize different grades or kinds of land occupancy, some of it being proprietorship and some of it tenancy and some of it mere shareholding. Thus far have we spoken of the partitioning of the land mostly in its large social and political relations; but to society also belongs the fertility of the land, and all efforts to conserve this fertility are public questions in the best sense. In America we think of tenant occupancy of land as dangerous because it does not safeguard fertility; in fact, it may waste fertility. This is because the practice in tenancy does not recognize the public interest in fertility, and the contract or agreement is made merely between the landowner and the tenant, and is largely an arrangement for skinning the land. It is only when the land itself is a party in the contract (when posterity is considered) that tenancy is safe. Then the tenant is obliged to fertilize the land, to practise certain rotations, and otherwise to conserve fertility, returning to the land the manurial value of products that are sold. When such contracts are made and enforced, tenancy farming does not deplete the land more than other farming, as the experience in some countries demonstrates. It is hardly to be expected, however, that tenant occupancy will give the man as close moral contact with the earth and its materials as will ownership; yet a well-developed tenancy is better than absentee farming by persons who live in town and run the farm by temporary hired help. The tenancy in the United States is partly a preliminary stage to ownership: if we can fulfil the moral obligation to society in the conserving of fertility and other natural resources, tenancy may be considered as a means to an end. Persons who work the land should have the privilege of owning it.

It may be urged by those who contend that land should be held by society, that this regulation of tenancy provides a means of administering all farm lands by government in the interest of maintenance of fertility. Leaving aside the primary desirability, as I see it, of reserving individual initiative, it is to be said that this kind of regulation of the tenant is possible only with a live-stock husbandry; nor do we yet have sufficient knowledge to enable us to project a legal system for all kinds of agriculture; nor again is it applicable to widely differing conditions and regions. A keener sense of responsibility will enable owner and tenant to work out better methods in all cases, but it is now impossible to incorporate complete control methods into successful legislative regulations. The increasing competition will make it ever more difficult for the careless man to make a good living by farming, and he will be driven from the business; or if he is not driven out, society will take away his privilege.

Yet we are not to think of society as founded wholly on small separate tracts, or "family farms," occupied by persons who live merely in contentment; this would mean that all landsmen would be essentially laborers. We need to hold on the land many persons who possess large powers of organization, who are managers, who can handle affairs in a bold way: it would be fatal to the best social and spiritual results if such persons could find no adequate opportunities on the land and were forced into other occupations. Undoubtedly we shall find ourselves with very unlike land units, encouraged and determined by the differing conditions and opportunities in different regions; and thereby shall we also avoid the great danger of making our fundamental occupation to produce a uniform and narrow class spirit.

We need the great example of persons who live separately on their lands, who desire to abide, who are serious in the business, and who have sufficient proprietary rights to enable them to handle the natural resources responsibly. There is a type of well-intentioned writers that would have the farmers live in centres in order that they may have what are called "social" advantages, betaking themselves every morning to the fields when the dew is on the grass and the birds sing, hastening back every evening (probably when the clock points to five) to engage in the delightful delirium of card-parties and moving-picture shows (of course gathering the golden harvest in the meantime). Other writers are to have the farms so small that the residences will be as close as on a village street, and a trolley-car will run through, and I suppose the band will play!

A new map

If, then, we are to give the people access to the holy earth, it means not only a new assent on the part of society but a new way of partitioning the surface. This is true whether we consider the subject wholly from the view-point of making natural resources utilizable or from the added desire to let the people out to those resources.

The organization of any affair or enterprise determines to a great extent the character of the result; and the organization rests directly on the subdivision into parts. The dividing of a business into separate responsibilities of different departments and sub-departments makes for easy access and for what we now know as efficiency; the dividing of a nation into states or provinces and counties and many lesser units makes political life possible; the setting off of a man's farm into fields, with lanes and roads connecting, makes a working enterprise. The more accurately these subdivisions follow natural and living necessities, the greater will be the values and the satisfactions that result from the undertaking.

Here is the open country, behind the great cities and the highly specialized industries. There are hills in it, great and small. There are forests here, none there; sands that nobody wants; fertile lands that everybody wants; shores inviting trade; mineral wealth; healing waters; power in streams; fish in ponds and lakes; building stone; swamps abounding in life; wild corners that stimulate desire; sceneries that take the soul into the far places. These are the fundamental reserves and the backgrounds. The first responsibility of any society is to protect them, husband them, bring them into use, and at the same time to teach the people what they mean.

40

A New Map

To bring them into use, and, at the same time, to protect them from rapacious citizens who have small social conscience, it is necessary to have good access. It is necessary to have roads. These roads should be laid where the resources exist, direct, purposeful. In a flat and uniform country, road systems may well be rectangular, following section-lines and intermediate lines; but the rectangularity is not the essential merit,—it is only a serviceable way of subdividing the resources. To find one's direction, north or south, is convenient, but it may clearly be subordinated to the utilization and protection of the supplies. The section-line division may accomplish this or it may not, and it is likely to place roads in wrong locations and to render the country monotonous and uninteresting.

But in the broken country, in the country of tumbled hills and crooked falling streams, of slopes that would better be left in the wild, and of lands that are good and fruitful for the plow, the roads may go the easy grades; but they ought also to go in such a plan as to open up the country to the best development, to divide its resources in the surest way for the greatest number of persons, and to reduce profitless human toil to the minimum,—and this is just what they may not do. They may go up over bare and barren hills merely to pass a few homesteads where no homesteads ought to be, roads that are always expensive and never good, that accomplish practically nothing for society. They leave good little valleys at one side, or enter them over almost impossible slopes. There are resources of physical wealth and of wonderful scenery that they do not touch, that would be of much value if they were accessible. The farming country is often not divided in such a way as to render it either most readily accessible or to make it the most useful as an asset for the people.

To connect villages and cities by stone roads is good. But what are we to do with all the back country, to make it contribute its needful part to feed the people in the days that are to come, and to open it to the persons who ought to go? We cannot accomplish this to the greatest purpose by the

41

present road systems, even if the roads themselves are all made good.

When the traveler goes to a strange country, he is interested in the public buildings, the cities, and some of the visible externals; but if he wants to understand the country, he must have a detailed map of its roads. The automobile maps are of no value for this purpose, for they show how one may pass over the country, not how the country is developed. As the last nerve-fibre and the last capillary are essential to the end of the finger and to the entire body, so the ultimate roads are essential to the myriad farms and to the national life. It is difficult in any country to get these maps, accurately and in detail; but they are the essential guidebooks.

We undertake great conquests of engineering, over mountains and across rivers and through the morasses; but at the last we shall call on the engineer for the greatest conquest of all,—how to divide the surface of the earth so that it shall yield us its best and mean to us the most, on the easiest grades, in the most practicable way, that we may utilize every piece of land to fullest advantage.

This means a new division and perhaps a redistribution of lands in such a way that the farmer will have his due proportion of hill and of valley, rather than that one shall have all valley and another all hard-scrabble on the hill or all waste land in some remote place. It means that there will be on each holding the proper relation of tilled land and pasture land and forest land, and that the outlets for the farmer and his products will be the readiest and the simplest that it is possible to make. It means that some roads will be abandoned entirely, as not worth the cost, and society will make a way for farmers living on impossible farms to move to other lands; and that there will be no "back roads," for they will be the marks of an undeveloped society. It means that we shall cease the pretense to bring all lands into farming, whether they are useful for farming or not; and that in the back country beyond the last farms there shall be trails that lead far away.

A New Map

In the farm region itself, much of the old division will pass away, being uneconomical and non-social. The abandonment of farms is in some cases a beginning of the process, but it is blind and undirected. Our educational effort is at present directed toward making the farmer prosperous on his existing farm, rather than to help him to secure a farm of proper resources and with proper access. As time goes on, we must reassemble many of the land divisions, if each man is to have adequate opportunity to make the most effective application of his knowledge, the best use of himself, and the greatest possible contribution to society. It would be well if some of the farms could be dispossessed of their owners, so that areas might be recombined on a better basis.

This is no Utopian or socialistic scheme, nor does it imply a forcible interference with vested rights. It is a plain statement of the necessities of the situation. Of course it cannot come about quickly or as a result of direct legislation; but there are various movements that may start it,—it is, in fact, already started. All the burning rural problems relate themselves in the end to the division of the land. In America, we do not suffer from the holding of the land in a few families or in an aristocratic class; that great danger we have escaped, but we have not yet learned how to give the land meaning to the greatest number of people. This is a question for the best political program, for we look for the day when statesmanship shall be expressed in the details of common politics.

We now hear much about the good-roads question, as if it were a problem only of highway construction: it is really a question of a new map.

The public program

It would be a great gain if many persons could look forward to the ownership of a bit of the earth, to share in the partition, to partake in the brotherhood. Some day we shall make it easy rather than difficult for this to be brought about.

Society, in its collective interest, also has necessities in the land. There is necessity of land to be owned by cities and other assemblages for water reservoirs, and all the rights thereto; for school grounds, playgrounds, reformatory institutions, hospitals, drill grounds, sewage-disposal areas, irrigation developments, drainage reclamations; for the public control of banks and borders of streams and ponds, for the shores of all vast bodies of water, for pleasure parks, recreation, breathing spaces in the great congestions, highways and other lines of communication; for the sites of public buildings, colleges and experiment stations, bird and beast refuges, fish and game reservations, cemeteries. There are also the rights of many semi-public agencies that need land,—of churches, of fraternal organizations, of incorporated seminaries and schools, of water-power and oil and coal developments, of manufacturing establishments, of extensive quarries, and of commercial enterprises of very many kinds. There is also the obligation of the general government that it shall have reserves against future needs, and that it shall protect the latent resources from exploitation and from waste. Great areas must be reserved for forests, as well as for other crops, and, in the nature of the case, these forest spaces in the future must be mostly in public ownership.

Great remainders should be held by the people to be sold in small parcels to those who desire to get out to the backgrounds but who do not want to be farmers, where they may spend a vacation or renew themselves in the soil or under the

44

trees, or by the green pastures or along the everlasting streams. It is a false assumption which supposes that if land cannot be turned into products of sale it is therefore valueless. The present active back-to-the-land movement has meaning to us here. It expresses the yearning of the people for contact with the earth and for escape from complexity and unessentials. As there is no regular way for attaining these satisfactions, it has largely taken the form of farming, which occupation has also been re-established in popular estimation in the same epoch. It should not be primarily a back-to-the-farm movement, however, and it is not to be derided. We are to recognize its meaning and to find some way of enabling more of the people to stand on the ground.

Aside from all this, land is needed for human habitation, where persons may have space and may have the privilege of gathering about them the goods that add value to life. Much land will be needed in future for this habitation, not only because there will be more people, but also because every person will be given an outlet. We know it is not right that any family should be doomed to the occupancy of a very few dreary rooms and deathly closets in the depths of great cities, seeing that all children are born to the natural sky and to the wind and to the earth. We do not yet see the way to allow them to have what is naturally theirs, but we shall learn how. In that day we shall take down the wonderful towers and cliffs in the cities, in which people work and live, shelf on shelf, but in which they have no home. The great city expansion in the end will be horizontal rather than perpendicular. We shall have many knots, clustered about factories and other enterprises, and we shall learn how to distribute the satisfactions in life rather than merely to assemble them. Before this time comes, we shall have passed the present insistence on so-called commercial efficiency, as if it were the sole measure of a civilization, and higher ends shall come to have control. All this will rest largely on the dividing of the land.

It is the common assumption that the solution of these problems lies in facilities of transportation, and, to an extent, this is true; but this assumption usually rests on the other assumption, that the method of the present city vortex is the method of all time, with its violent rush into the vortex and out of it, consuming vastly of time and energy, preventing home leisure and destroying locality feeling, herding the people like cattle. The question of transportation is indeed a major problem, but it must be met in part by a different philosophy of human effort, settling the people in many small or moderate assemblages rather than in a few mighty congestions. It will be better to move the materials than to move the people.

The great cities will grow larger; that is, they will cover more land. The smaller cities, the villages, the country towns will take on greatly increased importance. We shall learn how to secure the best satisfactions when we live in villages as well as when we live in cities. We begin to plan our cities and to a small extent our villages. We now begin to plan the layout of the farms, that they may accomplish the best results. But the cities and the towns depend on the country that lies beyond; and the country beyond depends on the city and the town. The problem is broadly one problem,—the problem of so dividing and subdividing the surface of the earth that there shall be the least conflict between all these interests, that public reservations shall not be placed where it is better to have farms, that farming developments may not interfere with public utilities, that institutions may be so placed and with such area as to develop their highest usefulness, that the people desiring outlet and contact with the earth in their own right may be accorded that essential privilege. We have not yet begun to approach the subject in a fundamental way, and yet it is the primary problem of the occupancy of the planet.

To the growing movement for city planning should be added an equal movement for country planning; and these should not proceed separately, but both together. No other public program is now more needed.

The honest day's work

There is still another application of this problem of the land background. It is the influence that productive ownership exerts on the day's work.

Yesterday for some time I observed eight working men engaged in removing parts of a structure and loading the pieces on a freight-car. At no time were more than two of the men making any pretension of working at once, most of the time they were all visiting or watching passers-by, and in the whole period the eight men did not accomplish what one good honest man should have performed. I wondered whether they had sufficient exercise to keep them in good health. They apparently were concerned about their "rights"; if the employer had rights they were undiscoverable.

We know the integrity and effectiveness of the body of workmen; yet any reader who has formed a habit of observing men on day work and public work will recognize my account. Day men usually work in gangs, frequently too many of them to allow any one to labor effectively, and the whole process is likely to be mechanical, impersonal, often shiftless and pervaded with the highly developed skill of putting in the time and reducing the time to the minimum and of beginning to quit well in advance of the quitting time. The process of securing labor has become involved, tied up, and the labor is not rendered in a sufficient spirit of service. About the only free labor yet remaining to us is the month labor on the farm, even though it may be difficult to secure and be comprised largely of ineffective remainders.

Over against all this is the importance of setting men at work singly and for themselves; this can be accomplished only when they own their property or have some real personal share

47

in the production. The gang-spirit of labor runs into the politics of the group and constitutes the norm. If we are to have self-acting men they must be removed from close control, in labor as well as elsewhere. If it is necessary that any great proportion of the laboring men shall be controlled, then is it equally important that other men in sufficient numbers shall constitute the requisite counterbalance and corrective. It is doubtful whether any kind of profit-sharing in closely controlled industries can ever be as effective in training responsible men for a democracy, other things being equal, as an occupation or series of occupations in which the worker is responsible for his own results rather than to an overseer, although the profit-sharing may for the time being develop the greater technical efficiency.

The influence of ownership on the performance of the man is often well illustrated when the farm laborer or tenant becomes the proprietor. Some of my readers will have had experience in the difficult and doubtful process of trying to "run a farm" at long range by means of ordinary hired help: the residence is uninhabitable; the tools are old and out of date, and some of them cannot be found; the well water is not good; the poultry is of the wrong breed, and the hens will not sit; the horses are not adapted to the work; the wagons must be painted and the harnesses replaced; the absolutely essential supplies are interminable; there must be more day labor. Now let this hired man come into the ownership of the farm: presto! the house can be repaired at almost no cost; the tools are good for some years yet; the harnesses can easily be mended; the absolutely essential supplies dwindle exceedingly; and the outside labor reduces itself to minor terms.

Work with machinery, in factories, may proceed more rapidly because the operator must keep up with the machine; and there are also definite standards or measures of performance. Yet even here it is not to be expected that the work will be much more than time-service. In fact, the very movement among labor is greatly to emphasize time-service, and often quite independently of justice. There must necessarily be a reaction from this attitude if we are to hope for the best human product.

The best human product results from the bearing of responsibility; in a controlled labor body the responsibility is shifted to the organization or to the boss. Assuredly the consolidating of labor is much to be desired if it is for the common benefit and for protection, and if it leaves the laborer free with his own product. Every person has the inalienable right to express himself, so long as it does not violate similar rights of his fellows, and to put forth his best production; if a man can best express himself in manual labor, no organization should suppress him or deny him that privilege. It is a sad case, and a denial of fundamental liberties, if a man is not allowed to work or to produce as much as he desires. Good development does not come from repression.

Society recognizes its obligation to the laboring man of whatever kind and the necessity of safeguarding him both in his own interest and because he stands at the very foundations; the laboring man bears an obligation to respond liberally with service and good-will.

Is it desirable to have an important part of the labor of a people founded on ownership? Is it worth while to have an example in a large class of the population of manual work that is free-spirited, and not dominated by class interest and time-service? Is it essential to social progress that a day's work shall be full measure?

The group reaction

One of the interesting phenomena of human association is the arising of a certain standard or norm of moral action within the various groups that compose it. These standards may not be inherently righteous, but they become so thoroughly established as to be enacted into law or even to be more powerful than law. So is it, as we have seen, with the idea of inalienable rights in natural property that may be held even out of all proportion to any proper use that the owners may be able to make of it; and so is it with the idea of inviolable natural privileges to those who control facilities that depend on public patronage for their commercial success. The man himself may hold one kind of personal morals, but the group of which he is a part may hold a very different kind. It is our problem, in dealing with the resources of the earth, to develop in the group the highest expression of duty that is to be found in individuals.

The restraint of the group, or the correction of the group action, is applied from the outside in the form of public opinion and in attack by other groups. The correction does not often arise from within. The establishing of many kinds of public-service bodies illustrates this fact. It is the check of society on group-selfishness.

These remarks apply to the man who stands at the foundation of society, next the earth, as well as to others, although he has not organized to propagate the action of his class. The spoliation of land, the insufficient regard for it, the trifling with it, is much more than an economic deficiency. Society will demand either through the pressure of public opinion, or by regularized action, that the producing power of the land shall be safeguarded and increased, as I have indicated in an

The Group Reaction

earlier part of the discussion. It will be better if it comes as the result of education, and thereby develops the voluntary feeling of obligation and responsibility. At the same time, it is equally the responsibility of every other person to make it possible for the farmer to prosecute his business under the expression of the highest standards.

There is just now abroad amongst us a teaching to the effect that the farmer cannot afford to put much additional effort into his crop production, inasmuch as the profit in an acre may not depend on the increase in yield, and therefore he does not carry an obligation to augment his acre-yields. This is a weakening philosophy.

Undoubtedly there is a point beyond which he may not go with profit in the effort to secure a heavy yield, for it may cost him too much to produce the maximum; so it may not be profitable for a transportation company to maintain the highest possible speed. With this economic question I have nothing to do; but it is the farmer's moral responsibility to society to increase his production, and the stimulation reacts powerfully upon himself. It is a man's natural responsibility to do his best: it is specially important that the man at the bottom put forth his best efforts. To increase his yields is one of the ways in which he expresses himself as a man and applies his knowledge. This incentive taken away, agriculture loses one of its best endeavors, the occupation remains stationary or even deteriorates, and society loses a moral support at the very point where it is most needed.

If the economic conditions are such that the farmer cannot afford to increase his production, then the remedy is to be found without rather than by the repression of the producer. We are expending vast effort to educate the farmer in the ways of better production, but we do not make it possible for him to apply this education to the best advantage.

The real farmer, the one whom we so much delight to honor, has a strong moral regard for his land, for his animals, and his crops. These are established men, with highly developed obligations, feeling their responsibility to the farm on which they live. No nation can long persist that does not have this kind of citizenry in the background.

I have spoken of one phase of the group reaction, as suggested in the attitude of the farmer. It may be interesting to recall, again, the fact that the purpose of farming is changing. The farmer is now adopting the outlook and the moral conduct of commerce. His business is no longer to produce the supplies for his family and to share the small overplus with society. He grows or makes a certain line of produce that he sells for cash, and then he purchases his other supplies in the general market. The days of homespun are gone. The farmer is as much a buyer as a seller. Commercial methods and standards are invading the remotest communities. This will have far-reaching results. Perhaps a fundamental shift in the moral basis of the agricultural occupations is slowly under way.

The measuring of farming in terms of yields and incomes introduces a dangerous standard. It is commonly assumed that State moneys for agriculture-education may be used only for "practical"—that is, for dollars-and-cents—results, and the emphasis is widely placed very exclusively on more alfalfa, more corn, more hogs, more fruit, on the two-blades-of-grass morals; and yet the highest good that can accrue to a State for the expenditure of its money is the raising up of a population less responsive to cash than to some other stimuli. The good physical support is indeed essential, but it is only the beginning of a process. I am conscious of a peculiar hardness in some of the agriculture-enterprise, with little real uplook; I hope that we may soon pass this cruder phase.

Undoubtedly we are in the beginning of an epoch in rural affairs. We are at a formative period. We begin to consider the rural problem increasingly in terms of social groups. The attitudes that these groups assume, the way in which they react to their problems, will be determined in the broader aspects for some time to come by the character of the young leadership that is now taking the field.

artificially created or developed

The spiritual contact with nature

A useful contact with the earth places man not as superior to nature but as a superior intelligence working in nature as a conscious and therefore as a responsible part in a plan of evolution, which is a continuing creation. It distinguishes the elemental virtues as against the acquired, factitious, and pampered virtues. These strong and simple traits may be brought out easily and naturally if we incorporate into our schemes of education the solid experiences of tramping, camping, scouting, farming, handcraft, and other activities that are not mere refinements of subjective processes.

Lack of training in the realities drives us to find satisfaction in all sorts of make-believes and in play-lives. The "movies" and many other developments of our time make an appeal wholly beyond their merits, and they challenge the methods and intentions of education. *outdoor vs indoor minds* *excessive amount*

There are more fundamental satisfactions than "thrills." There is more heart-ease in frugality than in surfeit. There is no real relish except when the appetite is keen. We are now provided with all sorts of things that nobody ever should want.

The good spiritual reaction to nature is not a form of dogmatism or impressionism. It results normally from objective experience, when the person is ready for it and has good digestion. It should be the natural emotion of the man who knows his objects and does not merely dream about them. There is no hallucination in it. The remedy for some of the erratic "futurism" and other forms of illusion is to put the man hard against the facts: he might be set to studying bugs or soils or placed between the handles of a plow until such time as objects begin to take their natural shape and meaning in his mind.

53

The Holy Earth

It is not within my purview here to consider the abstract righteous relation of man to the creation, nor to examine the major emotions that result from a contemplation of nature. It is only a very few of the simpler and more practical considerations that I may suggest.

The training in solid experience naturally emphasizes the righteousness of plain and simple eating and drinking, and of frugality and control in pleasures. Many of the adventitious pleasures are in the highest degree pernicious and are indications of weakness.

Considering the almost universal opinion that nature exhibits the merciless and relentless struggle of an eye for an eye and a tooth for a tooth, it is significant that one of the most productive ways of training a youth in sensitiveness and in regard for other creatures is by means of the nature contact. Even if the person is taught that the strong and ferocious survive and conquer, he nevertheless soon comes to have the tenderest regard for every living thing if he has the naturist in him. He discards the idea that we lose virility when we cease to kill, and relegates the notion to the limbo of deceits. This only means that unconsciously he has experienced the truth in nature, and in practice has discarded the erroneous philosophy contained in books even though he may still give these philosophies his mental assent.

It is exactly among the naturists that the old instinct to kill begins to lose its force and that an instinct of helpfulness and real brotherhood soon takes its place. From another source, the instinct to kill dies out among the moralists and other people. And yet it is passing strange how this old survival—or is it a reversion?—holds its place amongst us, even in the higher levels. The punishment of a life for a life is itself a survival. Entertainment even yet plays upon this old memory of killing, as in books of adventure, in fiction, in playgames of children, and worst of all on the stage where this strange anachronism, even in plays that are not historic, is still portrayed in pernicious features and in a way that would rouse any community and violate law if it were enacted in real life.

It is difficult to explain these survivals when we pretend to be so much shocked by the struggle for existence. We must accept the struggle, but we ought to try to understand it. The actual suffering among the creatures as the result of this struggle is probably small, and the bloody and ferocious contest that we like to picture to ourselves is relatively insignificant. There is a righteous element in the struggle; or, more truthfully, the struggle itself is right. Every living and sentient thing persists by its merit and by its right. It persists within its sphere, and usually not in the sphere of some other creature. The weeding-out process is probably related in some way with adaptability, but only remotely with physical strength. It is a process of applying the test. The test is applied continuously, and not in some violent upheaval.

If one looks for a moral significance in the struggle for existence, one finds it in the fact that it is a process of adjustment rather than a contest in ambition.

The elimination of the unessentials and of the survivals of a lower order of creation that have no proper place in human society, is the daily necessity of the race. The human struggle should not be on the plane of the struggle in the lower creation, by the simple fact that the human plane is unlike; and those who contend that we should draw our methods of contest from wild nature would therefore put us back on the plane of the creatures we are supposed to have passed. If there is one struggle of the creeping things, if there is one struggle of the fish of the sea and another of the beasts of the field, and still another of the fowls of the air, then surely there must be still another order for those who have dominion.

The struggle for existence: war

We may consider even further, although briefly, the nature of the struggle for existence in its spiritual relation. It would be violence to assume a holy earth and a holy production from the earth, if the contest between the creatures seems to violate all that we know as rightness.

The notion of the contentious and sanguinary struggle for existence finds its most pronounced popular expression in the existence of human war. It is a wide-spread opinion that war is necessary in the nature of things, and, in fact, it has been not only justified but glorified on this basis. We may here examine this contention briefly, and we may ask whether, in the case of human beings, there are other sufficient means of personal and social development than by mortal combat with one's fellows. We may ask whether the principle of enmity or the principle of fellow feeling is the more important and controlling.

We are not to deny or even to overlook the great results that have come from war. Virile races have forced themselves to the front and have impressed their stamp on society; the peoples have been mixed and also assorted; lethargic folk have been galvanized into activity; iron has been put into men's sinews; heroic deeds have arisen; old combinations and intrigues have been broken up (although new ones take their place). A kind of national purification may result from a great war. The state of human affairs has been brought to its present condition largely as the issue of wars.

On the other hand, we are not to overlook the damaging results, the destruction, the anguish, the check to all productive enterprise, the hatred and revenge, the hypocrisy and deceit, the despicable foreign spy system, the loss of standards, the demoralization, the lessening respect and regard for the rights of the other, the breeding of human parasites that fatten at the fringes of disaster, the levying of tribute, the setting up of unnatural boundaries, the thwarting of national and racial developments which, so far as we can see, gave every promise of great results. We naturally extol the nations that have survived; we do not know how many superior stocks may have been sacrificed to military conquest, or how many racial possibilities may have been suppressed in their beginnings.

Vast changes in mental attitudes may result from a great war, and the course of civilization may be deflected; and while we adjust ourselves to these changes, no one may say at the time that they are just or even that they are temporarily best. We are never able at the moment to measure the effects of the unholy conquest of peoples who should not have been conquered; these results work themselves out in tribulation and perhaps in loss of effort and of racial standards through many weary centuries. Force, or even "success," cannot justify theft.

But even assuming the great changes that have arisen from war, this is not a justification of war; it only states a fact, it only provides a measure of the condition of society at any epoch. It is probable that war will still exert a mighty even if a lessening influence; it may still be necessary to resort to arms to win for a people its natural opportunity and to free a race from bondage; and if any people has a right to its own existence, it has an equal right and indeed a duty to defend itself. But this again only indicates the wretched state of development in which we live. Undoubtedly, also, a certain amount of military training is very useful, but there should be other ways, in a democracy, to secure something of this needful training.

The struggle for existence, as expressed in human combat, does not necessarily result in the survival of the most desirable, so far as we are able to define desirability. We are confusing very unlike situations in our easy application of the struggle for existence to war. The struggle is not now between individuals to decide the fitter; it is between vast bodies hurling death by wholesale. We pick the physically fit and send them to the battle-line; and these fit are slain. This is not the situation in nature from which we draw our illustrations. Moreover, the final test of fitness in nature is adaptation, not power. Adaptation and adjustment mean peace, not war. Physical force has been immensely magnified in the human sphere; we even speak of the great nations as "powers," a terminology that some day we shall regret. The military method of civilization finds no justification in the biological struggle for existence.

The final conquest of a man is of himself, and he shall then be greater than when he takes a city. The final conquest of a society is of itself, and it shall then be greater than when it conquers its neighboring society.

Man now begins to measure himself against nature also, and he begins to see that herein shall lie his greatest conquests beyond himself; in fact, by this means shall he conquer himself,—by great feats of engineering, by completer utilization of the possibilities of the planet, by vast discoveries in the unknown, and by the final enlargement of the soul; and in these fields shall be the heroes. The most virile and upstanding qualities can find expression in the conquest of the earth. In the contest with the planet every man may feel himself grow.

What we have done in times past shows the way by which we have come; it does not provide a program of procedure for days that are coming; or if it does, then we deny the effective evolution of the race. We have passed witchcraft, religious persecution, the inquisition, subjugation of women, the enslavement of our fellows except alone enslavement in war.

Here I come particularly to a consideration of the struggle for existence. Before I enter on this subject, I must pause to say that I would not of myself found an argument either for war or against it on the analogies of the struggle for existence.

The Struggle for Existence: War

Man has responsibilities quite apart from the conditions that obtain in the lower creation. Man is a moral agent; animals and plants are not moral agents. But the argument for war is so often founded on this struggle in nature, that the question must be considered.

It has been persistently repeated for years that in nature the weakest perish and that the victory is with the strong, meaning by that the physically powerful. This is a false analogy and a false biology. It leads men far astray. It is the result of a misconception of the teaching of evolution.

Our minds dwell on the capture and the carnage in nature, —the hawk swooping on its prey, the cat stealthily watching for the mouse, wolves hunting in packs, ferocious beasts lying in wait, sharks that follow ships, serpents with venomous fangs, the vast range of parasitism; and with the poet we say that nature is "red in tooth and claw." Of course, we are not to deny the struggle of might against might, which is mostly between individuals, and of which we are all aware; but the weak and the fragile and the small are the organisms that have persisted. There are thousands of little and soft things still abundant in the world that have outlived the fearsome ravenous monsters of ages past; there were Goliaths in those days, but the Davids have outlived them, and Gath is not peopled by giants. The big and strong have not triumphed.

The struggle in nature is not a combat, as we commonly understand that word, and it is not warfare. The earth is not strewn with corpses.

I was impressed in reading Roosevelt's "African Game Trails" with the great extent of small and defenseless and fragile animal life that abounds in the midst of the terrible beasts,—little uncourageous things that hide in the crevices, myriads that fly in the air, those that ride on the rhinos, that swim and hide in the pools, and bats that hang in the acacia-trees. He travelled in the region of the lion, in the region that "holds the mightiest creatures that tread the earth or swim in its rivers; it also holds distant kinsfolk of these same creatures, no bigger than woodchucks, which dwell in crannies of the rocks, and in the tree tops. There are antelope smaller than hares and antelope larger than oxen. There are creatures which are the embodiment of grace; and others whose huge ungainliness is like that of a shape in a nightmare. The plains are alive with droves of strange and beautiful animals whose life is not known elsewhere." The lion is mighty; he is the king of beasts; but he keeps his place and he has no kingdom. He has not mastered the earth. No beast has ever overcome the earth; and the natural world has never been conquered by muscular force.

Nature is not in a state of perpetual enmity, one part with another.

My friend went to a far country. He told me that he was most impressed with the ferocity, chiefly of wild men. It came my time to go to that country. I saw that men had been savage,—men are the most ferocious of animals, and the ferocity has never reached its high point of refined fury until today. (Of course, savages fight and slay; this is because they are savages.) But I saw also that these savage men are passing away. I saw animals that had never tasted blood, that had no means of defense against a rapacious captor, and yet they were multiplying. Every stone that I upturned disclosed some tender organism; every bush that I disturbed revealed some timid atom of animal life; every spot where I walked bore some delicate plant, and I recalled the remark of Sir J. William Dawson "that frail and delicate plants may be more ancient than the mountains or plains on which they live"; and if I went on the sea, I saw the medusae, as frail as a poet's dream, with the very sunshine streaming through them, yet holding their own in the mighty upheaval of the oceans; and I reflected on the myriads of microscopic things that for untold ages had cast the very rock on which much of the ocean rests. The minor things and the weak things are the most numerous, and they have played the greatest part in the polity of nature. So I came away from that far country impressed with the power of the little feeble things. I had a new understanding of the worth of creatures so unobtrusive and so silent that the multitude does not know them.

I saw protective colorings; I saw fleet wings and swift feet; I saw the ability to hide and to conceal; I saw habits of adaptation; I saw marvellous powers of reproduction. You have seen them in every field; you have met them on your casual walks, until you accept them as the natural order of things. And you know that the beasts of prey have not prevailed. The whole contrivance of nature is to protect the weak.

We have wrongly visualized the "struggle." We have given it an intensely human application. We need to go back to Darwin who gave significance to the phrase "struggle for existence." "I use this term," he said, "in a large and metaphorical sense, including dependence of one being on another, and including (which is more important) not only the life of the individual, but success in leaving progeny." The dependence of one being on another, success in leaving progeny,—how accurate and how far-seeing was Darwin!

I hope that I speak to naturists and to farmers. They know how diverse are the forms of life; and they know that somehow these forms live together and that only rarely do whole races perish by subjugation. They know that the beasts do not set forth to conquer, but only to gain subsistence and to protect themselves. The beasts and birds do not pursue indiscriminately. A hen-hawk does not attack crows or butterflies. Even a vicious bull does not attack fowls or rabbits or sheep. The great issues are the issues of live and let-live. There are whole nations of plants, more unlike than nations of humankind, living together in mutual interdependence. There are nations of quiet and mightless animals that live in the very regions of the mighty and the stout. And we are glad it is so.

Consider the mockery of invoking the struggle for existence as justification for a battle on a June morning, when all nature is vibrant with life and competition is severe, and when, if ever, we are to look for strife. But the very earth breathes peace. The fulness of every field and wood is in complete adjustment. The teeming multitudes of animal and plant have found a way to live together, and we look abroad on a vast harmony, verdurous, prolific, abounding. Into this concord, project your holocaust!

Reading Nature and reading the Bible must proceed similarly. We can use a narrow slice in each case to "support" any point. We can dismiss the message of each by claiming to see inconsistencies or brutalities. Or we can discern a wider context and see the grand sweep: sustainability and eternity rest in adaptation to a given shalom.

JLH

The daily fare

Some pages back, I said something about the essential simplicity in habit of life that results from the nature contact, and I illustrated the remark by calling attention to the righteousness of simple eating and drinking. Of course, the eating must be substantial, but the adventitious appetites accomplish nothing and they may be not only intemperate and damaging to health but even unmoral. Yet it is not alone the simplicity of the daily fare that interests me here, but the necessity that it shall be as direct as possible from the ground or the sea, and that it shall be undisguised and shall have meaning beyond the satisfying of the appetite.

I was interested in Tusser's "Christmas husbandly fare," notwithstanding some suggestion of gluttony in it and of oversupply. There is a certain vigor and good relish about it, and lack of ostentation, that seem to suggest a lesson.

It was more than three centuries ago that native Thomas Tusser, musician, chorister, and farmer, gave to the world his incomparable "Five Hundred Points of Good Husbandry." He covered the farm year and the farm work as completely as Vergil had covered it more than fifteen centuries before; and he left us sketches of the countryside of his day, and the ways of the good plain folk, and quaint bits of philosophy and counsel. He celebrated the Christmas festival with much conviction, and in the homely way of the home folks, deriving his satisfactions from the things that the land produces. His sketches are wholesome reading in these days of foods transported from the ends of the earth, and compounded by impersonal devices and condensed into packages that go into every house alike.

Thomas Tusser would celebrate with "things handsome to

have, as they ought to be had." His board would not be scant of provisions, for he seems not to have advised the simple life in the way of things good to eat; but he chose good raw materials, and we can imagine that the "good husband and huswife" gave these materials their best compliments and prepared them with diligence and skill. Not once does he suggest that these materials be secured from the market, or that any imported labor be employed in the preparation of them.

> Good bread and good drink, a good fire in the hall,
> Brawn, pudding, and souse, and good mustard withal.

Here is the whole philosophy of the contented festival,—the fruit of one's labor, the common genuine materials, and the cheer of the family fireside. The day is to be given over to the spirit of the celebration; every common object will glow with a new consecration, and everything will be good,—even the mustard will be good withal. What a contempt old Tusser would have had for all the imported and fabricated condiments and trivialities that now come to our tables in packages suggestive of medicines and drugs! And how ridiculously would they have stood themselves beside the brawn, pudding, and souse! A few plain accessories, every one stout and genuine, and in good quantity, must accompany the substantialities that one takes with a free hand directly from the land that one manages.

It surprises us that he had such a bountiful list from which to draw, and yet the kinds are not more than might be secured from any good land property, if one set about securing them:

> Beef, mutton, and pork, shred pies of the best,
> Pig, veal, goose, and capon, and turkey well drest,
> Cheese, apples, and nuts, joly carols to hear,
> As then in the country, is counted good cheer.

In these days we should draw less heavily on the meats, for in the three centuries we have gained greatly in the vegetable foods. Tusser did not have the potato. But nevertheless, these materials are of the very bone of the land. They grow up with the year and out of the conditions, and they have all the days in them, the sunshine, the rain, the dew of morning, the wind, the cold foggy nights, and the work of laborious hands. Every one of them means something to the person who raises them, and there is no impersonality in them. John's father drained the land when yet he was a boy; the hedges were set; long ago the place was laid out in its rotations; the old trees in the fields are a part of it; every stall in the stables and every window-seat in the old house hold memories; and John has grown up with these memories, and with these fields, and with the footpaths that lead out over brooks and amongst the herds of cattle. It is a part of his religion to keep the land well; and these supplies at Christmas time are taken with a deep reverence for the goodness that is in them, and with a pride in having produced them.

And Thomas Tusser, good husbandman, rejoiced that these bounties cost no cash:

> What cost to good husband, is any of this?
> Good household provision only it is.
> Of other the like, I do leave out a many
> That costeth a husbandman never a penny.

To farm well; to provide well; to produce it oneself; to be independent of trade, so far as this is possible in the furnishing of the table,—these are good elements in living. And in this day we are rapidly losing all this; many persons already have lost it; many have never known the satisfaction of it. Most of us must live from the box and the bottle and the tin-can; we are even feeding our cattle from the factory and the bag. The farmer now raises a few prime products to sell, and then he buys his foods in the markets under label and tag; and he knows not who produced the materials, and he soon comes not to care. No thought of the seasons, and of the men and women who labored, of the place, of the kind of soil, of the special contribution of the native earth, come with the trademark or the brand. And so we all live mechanically, from shop to table, without contact, and irreverently.

The Holy Earth

May we not once in the year remember the earth in the food that we eat? May we not in some way, even though we live in town, so organize our Christmas festival that the thought of the goodness of the land and its bounty shall be a conscious part of our celebration? May we not for once reduce to the very minimum the supply of manufactured and sophisticated things, and come somewhere near, at least in spirit, to a "Christmas husbandly fare?"

Yet, Thomas Tusser would not confine his husbandly fare to the Christmas time. In another poem, he gives us "The farmer's daily diet," in which the sturdy products are still much the same, secured and prepared by those who partake. All this may be little applicable literally in our present living, and yet I think it is easily possible, as certainly it is very desirable, to develop a new attitude toward the table fare, avoiding much unnecessary and insignificant household labor and lending an attitude of good morality to the daily sustenance.

Much of our eating and feasting is a vicious waste of time, and also of human energy that might be put to good uses. One can scarcely conceive how such indirect and uncomfortable and expensive methods could have come into use. Perhaps they originated with persons of quality in an aristocratic society, when an abundance of servants must be trained to serve and when distinctions in eating were a part of the distinction in rank. But to have introduced these laborious and unintelligent methods into hotels, where persons tarry for comfort and into homes that do not need to maintain an extrinsic appearance, is a vain and ludicrous imitation. The numbers of courses, with more service than food, that one often meets at the table d'hote of the frequented hotels abroad, are most exasperating to one who values time and has a serious purpose in travel and a rightful care for the bodily apparatus. Here is the performance—it was nothing more than a performance, consisting in repeated changing of all the dishes, the removing of every fragment of edibles, and in passing very small separate parcels of food—that it was my lot to endure on an otherwise happy day in a hotel that had little else to distinguish it:

Course 1. Dry bread (no butter).
            Removal.

Course 2. Soup (nothing else).
            Removal.

Course 3. Fish (very economical), with a potato on the side.
            Removal.

Course 4. Veal, macaroni.
            Removal.

Course 5. Spoonful of green beans (nothing else).
            Removal.

Course 6. Beef and salad (fragmentary).
            Removal.

Course 7. Charlotte Russe, bit of cake.
            Removal.

Course 8. Fruit (slight).
            Removal.

Course 9. Morsel of cheese, one cracker.
            Removal.

Course 10. Coffee.
            Relief.

The traveler knows that this species of time-wasting is not unusual; certainly the food is not unusual and does not merit such considerate attention, although it may profit by the magnification. All this contributes nothing to human efficiency—quite the reverse—and certainly nothing to the rightful gusto in the enjoyment of one's subsistence. It is a ceremony. Such laborious uselessness is quite immoral.

I am afraid that our food habits very well represent how far we have moved away from the essentials and how much we have misled ourselves as to the standards of excellence. I looked in a cookbook to learn how to serve potatoes: I found twenty-three recipes, every one of which was apparently designed to disguise the fact that they were potatoes; and yet there is really nothing in a potato to be ashamed of. Of course, this kind of deception is not peculiar to cookery. It is of the same piece as the stamping of the metal building coverings in forms to represent brick and stone, although everybody knows that they are not brick and stone, rather than to make a design that shall express metal and thereby frankly tell the truth; of the same kind also as the casting of cement blocks to represent undressed rock, although every one is aware of the deception, rather than to develop a form that will express cement blocks as brick expresses brick; of the same order as the inflating of good wholesome water by carbonic gas; and all the other deceits in materials on which our common affairs are built. It is, of course, legitimate to present our foods in many forms that we may secure variety even with scant and common materials; but danger may lie in any untruthfulness with which we use the raw materials of life.

So cookery has come to be a process of concealment. Not only does it conceal the materials, but it also conceals the names of them in a ridiculous nomenclature. Apparently, the higher the art of cookery, the greater is the merit of complete concealment. I think that one reason why persons enjoy the simple cooking of farmers and sailors and other elemental folk, is because of its comparative lack of disguise, although they may not be aware of this merit of it. We have so successfully disguised our viands through so many years that it is not "good form" to make inquiries: we may not smell the food, although the odor should be one of the best and most rightful satisfactions, as it is in fruits and flowers. We may smell a parsnip or a potato when it grows in the field, but not when it is cooked.

We add the extrinsic and meaningless odors of spices and flavorings, forgetting that odor no less than music hath occasions; each of the materials has its own odor that the discriminating cook will try to bring out in its best expression. Were we to be deprived of all these exotic seasonings, undoubtedly cookery would be the gainer in the end; nor could we so readily disguise materials that in themselves are not fit to eat.

The Daily Fare

There is a reason why "all foods taste alike," as we often hear it said of the cooking in public places.

Moreover, we want everything that is out of season, necessitating great attention to the arts of preserving and requiring still further fabrication; and by this desire we also lessen the meaning of the seasons when they come in their natural sequence, bringing their treasure of materials that are adapted to the time and to the place. We can understand, then, why it so happens that we neglect the cookery of the common foods, as seeming to be not quite worth the while, and expend ourselves with so much effort on the accessories and the frills. I have been interested to observe some of the instruction in cooking,—how it often begins with little desserts, and fudge, and a variety of dib-dabs. This is much like the instruction in manual training that begins with formal and meaningless model work or trivialities and neglects the issues of life. It is much like some of the teaching in agriculture not so many years ago, before we attacked very effectively the serious problems of wheat and alfalfa and forests and markets. Mastery does not lie in these pieces of play work, nor does the best intellectual interest on the part of the student reside in them.

Result is that one finds the greatest difficulty in securing a really good baked potato, a well-cooked steak, or a wholesome dish of apple-sauce that is not strained and flavored beyond recognition. It is nearly impossible for one to secure an egg fried hard and yet very tender and that has not been "turned" or scorched on the edges,—this is quite the test of the skill of the good cook. The notion that a hard fried egg is dangerously indigestible is probably a fable of poor cookery. One can secure many sophisticated and disguised egg dishes, but I think skill in plainly cooking eggs is almost an unknown art, perhaps a little-practised art.

Now, it is on these simple and essential things that I would start my instruction in cookery; and this not only for the gain to good eating but also for the advantage of vigor and good morals. I am afraid that our cooking does not set a good example before the young three times every day in the year; and how eager are the young and how amenable to suggestion at these three blessed epochs every day in the year!

Some unsympathetic reader will say that I am drawing a long bow; yet undoubtedly our cookery has prepared the public mind for the adulteration. Knowing the elaboration of many of the foods and fancy dishes, the use of flavoring and spice and other additions to disguise unwholesome materials, the addition of coloring matter to make things attractive, the mixtures, the elaborate designs and trimmings and concoctions, and various deceptions, one wonders how far is the step from some of the cookery to some of the adulteration and whether these processes are really all of one piece. I will leave with my reader a paragraph assembled from a statement made by a food chemist but a few years ago, to let him compare adulteration with what is regarded as legitimate food preparation and note the essential similarity of many of the processes. I do not mean to enter the discussion of food adulteration, and I do not know whether these sophistications are true at the present day; but the statement describes a situation in which we found ourselves and indicates what had become a staggering infidelity in the use of the good raw materials.

Hamburg steak often contains sodium sulphite; bologna sausage and similar meats until recently usually contained a large percentage of added cereal. "Pancake flour" often contains little if any buckwheat; wheat flour is bleached with nitric oxide to improve its appearance. Fancy French peas are colored with sulphate of copper. Bottled ketchup usually contains benzoate of soda as a preservative. Japanese tea is colored with cyanide of potassium and iron. Prepared mustard usually contains a large quantity of added starch and is colored with tumeric. Ground coffee has recently been adulterated with roasted peas. So-called non-alcoholic bottled beverages often contain alcohol or a habit-forming drug and are usually colored with aniline. Candy is commonly colored with aniline dye and often coated with paraffine to prevent evaporation. Cheap candies contain such substances as glue and soapstone. The higher-priced kinds of molasses usually contain sulphites. Flavoring extracts seldom are made from pure products and usually are artificially colored. Jams are made of apple jelly with the addition of coloring matter and also of seeds to imitate berries from which they are supposed to be made; the cheap apple jelly is itself often imitated by a mixture of glucose, starch, aniline dye, and flavoring. Lard nearly always contains added tallow. Bakeries in large cities have used decomposed products, as decayed eggs. Cheap ice-cream is often made of gelatin, glue, and starch. Cottonseed-oil is sold for olive-oil. The poison saccharine is often used in place of sugar in prepared sweetened products.

The attentive reader of the public prints in the recent years can greatly extend this humiliating recital if he choose. It is our habit to attach all the blame to the adulterators, and it is difficult to excuse them; but we usually find that there are contributory causes and certainly there must be reasons. Has our daily fare been honest?

The admiration of good materials

Not even yet am I done with this plain problem of the daily fare. The very fact that it is daily—thrice daily—and that it enters so much into the thought and effort of every one of us, makes it a subject of the deepest concern from every point of view. The aspect of the case that I am now to reassert is the effect of much of our food preparation in removing us from a knowledge of the good raw materials that come out of the abounding earth.

Let us stop to admire an apple. I see a committee of the old worthies in some fruit-show going slowly and discriminatingly among the plates of fruits, discussing the shapes and colors and sizes, catching the fragrance, debating the origins and the histories, and testing them with the utmost precaution and deliberation; and I follow to hear their judgment.

This kind of apple is very perfect in spherical form, deeply cut at the stem, well ridged at the shallow crater, beautifully splashed and streaked with carmine-red on a yellowish green under-color, finely flecked with dots, slightly russet on the shaded side, apparently a good keeper; its texture is fine-grained and uniform, flavor mildly subacid, the quality good to very good; if the tree is hardy and productive, this variety is to be recommended to the amateur for further trial! The next sample is somewhat elongated in form, rather below the average in color, the stem very long and well set and indicating a fruit that does not readily drop in windstorms, the texture exceedingly melting but the flavor slightly lacking in character and therefore rendering it of doubtful value for further test. Another sample lacks decidedly in quality, as judged by the specimens on the table, and the exhibitor is respectfully recommended to withdraw it from future exhibi-

72

tions; another kind has a very pronounced aromatic odor, which will commend it to persons desiring to grow a choice collection of interesting fruits; still another is of good size, very firm and solid, of uniform red color, slightly oblate and therefore lending itself to easy packing, quality fair to good, and if the tree bears such uniform samples as those shown on the table it apparently gives promise of some usefulness as a market sort. My older friends, if they have something of the feeling of the pomologist, can construct the remainder of the picture.

In physical perfectness of form and texture and color, there is nothing in all the world that exceeds a well-grown fruit. Let it lie in the palm of your hand. Close your fingers slowly about it. Feel its firm or soft and modelled surface. Put it against your cheek, and inhale its fragrance. Trace its neutral under-colors, and follow its stripes and mark its dots. If an apple, trace the eye that lies in a moulded basin. Note its stem, how it stands firmly in its cavity, and let your imagination run back to the tree from which, when finally mature, it parted freely. This apple is not only the product of your labor, but it holds the essence of the year and it is in itself a thing of exquisite beauty. There is no other rondure and no other fragrance like this.

I am convinced that we need much to cultivate this appreciation of the physical perfectness of the fruits that we grow. We cannot afford to lose this note from our lives, for this may contribute a good part of our satisfaction of being in the world. The discriminating appreciation that one applies to a picture or a piece of sculpture may be equally applied to any fruit that grows on the commonest tree or bush in our field or to any animal that stands on a green pasture. It is no doubt a mark of a well-tempered mind that it can understand the significance of the forms in fruits and plants and animals and apply it in the work of the day.

I sometimes think that the rise of the culinary arts is banishing this fine old appreciation of fruits in their natural forms. There are so many ways of canning and preserving and evaporating and extracting the juices, so many disguises and so much fabrication, that the fruit is lost in the process. The tin-can and the bottle seem to have put an insuperable barrier between us and nature, and it is difficult for us to get back to a good munch of real apples under a tree or by the fireside. The difficulty is all the greater in our congested city life where orchards and trees are only a vacant memory or stories told to the young, and where the space in the larder is so small that apples must be purchased by the quart. The eating of good apples out of hand seems to be almost a lost art. Only the most indestructible kinds, along with leather-skinned oranges and withered bananas, seem to be purchasable in the market. The discriminating apple-eater in the Old World sends to a grower for samples of the kinds that he grows; and after the inquirer has tested them in the family, and discussed them, he orders his winter supply. The American leaves the matter to the cook and she orders plain apples; and she gets them.

I wonder whether in time the perfection of fabrication will not reach such a point that some fruits will be known to the great public only by the picture on the package or on the bottle. Every process that removes us one step farther from the earth is a distinct loss to the people, and yet we are rapidly coming into the habit of taking all things at second hand. My objection to the wine of the grape is not so much a question of abstinence as of the fact that I find no particular satisfaction in the shape and texture of a bottle.

If one has a sensitive appreciation of the beauty in form and color and modelling of the common fruits, he will find his interest gradually extending to other products. Some time ago I visited Hood River Valley in company with a rugged potato-grower from the Rocky Mountains. We were amazed at the wonderful scenery, and captivated by the beauty of the fruits. In one orchard the owner showed us with much satisfaction a brace of apples of perfect form and glowing colors. When the grower had properly expounded the marvels of

The Admiration of Good Materials

Hood River apples, which he said were the finest in the world, my friend thrust his hand into his pocket and pulled out a potato, and said to the man: "Why is not that just as handsome as a Hood River apple?" And sure enough it was. For twenty-five years this grower had been raising and selecting the old Peachblow potato, until he had a form much more perfect than the old Peachblow ever was, with a uniform delicate pink skin, smooth surface, comely shape, and medium size, and with eyes very small and scarcely sunken; and my Hood River friend admitted that a potato as well as an apple may be handsome and satisfying to the hand and to the eye, and well worth carrying in one's pocket. But this was a high-bred potato, and not one of the common lot.

This episode of the potato allows me another opportunity to enforce my contention that we lose the fruit or the vegetable in the processes of cookery. The customary practice of "mashing" potatoes takes all the individuality out of the product, and the result is mostly so much starch. There is an important dietary side to this. Cut a thin slice across a potato and hold it to the light. Note the interior undifferentiated mass, and then the thick band of rind surrounding it. The potato flavor and a large part of the nutriment lie in this exterior. We slice this part away and fry, boil, or otherwise fuss up the remainder. When we mash it, we go still farther and break down the potato texture; and in the modern method we squeeze and strain it till we eliminate every part of the potato, leaving only a pasty mass, which, in my estimation, is not fit to eat. The potato should be cooked with the rind on, if it is a good potato, and if it is necessary to remove the outer skin the process should be performed after the cooking. The most toothsome part of the potato is in these outer portions, if the tuber is well grown and handled. We have so sophisticated the potato in the modern disguised cookery that we often practically ruin it as an article of food, and we have bred a race of people that sees nothing to admire in a good and well-grown potato tuber.

The Holy Earth

I now wish to take an excursion from the potato to the pumpkin. In all the range of vegetable products, I doubt whether there is a more perfect example of pleasing form, fine modelling, attractive texture and color, and more bracing odor, than in a well-grown and ripe field pumpkin. Place a pumpkin on your table; run your fingers down its smooth grooves; trace the furrows to the poles; take note of its form; absorb its rich color; get the tang of its fragrance. The roughness and ruggedness of its leaves, the sharp-angled stem strongly set, make a foil that a sculptor cannot improve. Then wonder how this marvellous thing was born out of your garden soil through the medium of one small strand of a succulent stem.

We all recognize the appeal of a bouquet of flowers, but we are unaware that we may have a bouquet of fruits. We have given little attention to arranging them, or any study of the kinds that consort well together, nor have we receptacles in which effectively to display them. Yet, apples and oranges and plums and grapes and nuts, and good melons and cucumbers and peppers and carrots and onions, may be arranged into the most artistic and satisfying combinations.

I would fall short of my obligation if I were to stop with the fruit of the tree and say nothing about the tree or the plant itself. In our haste for lawn trees of new kinds and from the uttermost parts, we forget that a fruit-tree is ornamental and that it provides acceptable shade. A full-grown apple-tree or pear-tree is one of the most individual and picturesque of trees. The foliage is good, the blossoms as handsome as those of fancy imported things, the fruits always interesting, and the tree is reliable. Nothing is more interesting than an orange tree, in the regions where it grows, with its shining and evergreen leaves and its continuing flowers and fruits. The practice of planting apples and pears and sweet cherries, and other fruit and nut trees, for shade and adornment is much to be commended in certain places.

But the point I wish specially to urge in this connection is the value of many kinds of fruit-trees in real landscape work. We think of these trees as single or separate specimens, but they may be used with good result in mass planting, when it is desired to produce a given effect in a large area or in one division of a property. I do not know that any one has worked out full plans for the combining of fruit-trees, nuts, and berry-bearing plants into good treatments, but it is much to be desired that this shall be done. Any of you can picture a sweep of countryside planted to these things that would be not only novel and striking, but at the same time conformable to the best traditions of artistic rendering.

I think it should be a fundamental purpose in our educational plans to acquaint the people with the common resources of the region, and particularly with those materials on which we subsist. If this is accepted, then we cannot deprive our parks, highways, and school grounds of the trees that bear the staple fruits. It is worth while to have an intellectual interest in a fruit-tree. I know a fruit-grower who secures many prizes for his apples and his pears; when he secures a blue ribbon, he ties it on the tree that bore the fruit.

The admiration of a good domestic animal is much to be desired. It develops a most responsible attitude in the man or the woman. I have observed a peculiar charm in the breeders of these wonderful animals, a certain poise and masterfulness and breadth of sympathy. To admire a good horse and to know just why he admires him is a great resource to any man, as also to feel the responsibility for the care and health of any flock or herd. Fowls, pigs, sheep on their pastures, cows, mules, all perfect of their kind, all sensitive, all of them marvellous in their forms and powers,—verily these are good to know.

If the raw materials grow out of the holy earth, then a man should have pride in producing them, and also in handling them. As a man thinketh of his materials, so doth he profit in the use of them. He builds them into himself. There is a widespread feeling that in some way these materials reflect themselves in a man's bearing. One type of man grows out of the handling of rocks, another out of the handling of fishes, another out of the growing of the products from the good earth. All irreverence in the handling of these materials that come out of the earth's bounty, and all waste and poor workmanship, make for a low spiritual expression.

The farmer specially should be proud of his materials, he is so close to the sources and so hard against the backgrounds. Moreover, he cannot conceal his materials. He cannot lock up his farm or disguise his crops. He lives on his farm, and visibly with his products. The architect does not live in the houses and temples he builds. The engineer does not live on his bridge. The miner does not live in his mine. Even the sailor has his home away from his ship. But the farmer cannot separate himself from his works. Every bushel of buckwheat and every barrel of apples and every bale of cotton bears his name; the beef that he takes to market, the sheep that he herds on his pastures, the horse that he drives,—these are his products and they carry his name. He should have the same pride in these—his productions—as another who builds a machine, or another who writes a book about them. The admiration of a field of hay, of a cow producing milk, of a shapely and fragrant head of cabbage, is a great force for good.

It would mean much if we could celebrate the raw materials and the products. Particularly is it good to celebrate the yearly bounty. The Puritans recognized their immediate dependence on the products of the ground, and their celebration was connected with religion. I should be sorry if our celebrations were to be wholly secular.

We have been much given to the display of fabricated materials,—of the products of looms, lathes, foundries, and many factories of skill. We also exhibit the agricultural produce, but largely in a crass and rude way to display bulk and to win prizes. We now begin to arrange our exhibitions for color effect, comparison, and educational influence. But we do not justly understand the natural products when we confine them to formal exhibitions. They must be incorporated into many celebrations, expressing therein the earth's bounty and our appreciation of it. The usual and common products, domesticated and wild, should be gathered in these occasions, and not for competition or for prize awards or even for display, but for their intrinsic qualities. An apple day or an apple sabbath would teach the people to express their gratitude for apples. The moral obligation to grow good apples, to handle them honestly, to treat the soil and the trees fairly and reverently, could be developed as a living practical philosophy into the working-days of an apple-growing people. The technical knowledge we now possess requires the moral support of a stimulated public appreciation to make it a thoroughly effective force.

Many of the products and crops lend themselves well to this kind of admiration, and all of them should awaken gratitude and reverence. Sermons and teaching may issue from them. Nor is it necessary that this gratitude be expressed only in collected materials, or that all preaching and all teaching shall be indoors. The best understanding of our relations to to the earth will be possible when we learn how to apply our devotions in the open places.

The keeping of the beautiful earth

The proper care-taking of the earth lies not alone in maintaining its fertility or in safeguarding its products. The lines of beauty that appeal to the eye and the charm that satisfies the five senses are in our keeping.

The natural landscape is always interesting and it is satisfying. The physical universe is the source of art. We know no other form and color than that which we see in nature or derive from it. If art is true to its theme, it is one expression of morals. If it is a moral obligation to express the art-sense in painting and sculpture and literature and music, so is it an equal obligation to express it in good landscape.

Of the first importance is it that the race keep its artistic backgrounds, and not alone for the few who may travel far and near and who may pause deliberately, but also for those more numerous folk who must remain with the daily toil and catch the far look only as they labor. To put the best expression of any landscape into the consciousness of one's day's work is more to be desired than much riches. When we complete our conquest, there will be no unseemly landscapes.

The abundance of violated landscapes is proof that we have not yet mastered. The farmer does not have full command of his situation until the landscape is a part of his farming. Farms may be units in well-developed and pleasing landscapes, beautiful in their combinations with other farms and appropriate to their setting as well as attractive in themselves.

No one has a moral right to contribute unsightly factory premises or a forbidding commercial establishment to any community. The lines of utility and efficiency ought also to be the lines of beauty; and it is due every worker to have a good landscape to look upon, even though its area be very constricted. To produce bushels of wheat and marvels of machinery, to maintain devastating military establishments, do not comprise the sum of conquest. The backgrounds must be kept.

If moral strength comes from good and sufficient scenery, so does the preservation of it become a social duty. It is much more than a civic obligation. But the resources of the earth must be available to man for his use and this necessarily means a modification of the original scenery. Some pieces and kinds of scenery are above all economic use and should be kept wholly in the natural state. Much of it may yield to modification if he takes good care to preserve its essential features. Unfortunately, the engineer seems not often to be trained in the values of scenery and he is likely to despoil a landscape or at least to leave it raw and unfinished.

On the other hand, there is unfortunately a feeling abroad that any modification of a striking landscape is violation and despoliation; and unwarranted opposition, in some cases amounting almost to prudery, follows any needful work of utilization. Undoubtedly the farmer and builder and promoter have been too unmindful of the effect of their interference on scenery, and particularly in taking little care in the disposition of wastes and in the healing of wounds; but a work either of farming or of construction may add interest and even lines of beauty to a landscape and endow it with the suggestion of human interest. If care were taken in the construction of public and semi-public work to reshape the banks into pleasing lines, to clean up, to care for, to plant, to erect structures of good proportions whether they cost much or little, and to give proper regard to the sensibilities of the communities, most of the present agitation against interference with natural scenery would disappear. One has only to visit the factory districts, the vacation resorts, the tenement areas, the banks of streams and gorges, to look at the faces of cliffs and at many engineering enterprises and at numberless farmyards, to find examples of the disregard of men for the materials that they handle. It is as much our obligation to hold the scenery reverently as to handle the products reverently. Man found the earth looking well. Humanity began in a garden.

The keeping of the good earth depends on preservation rather than on destruction. The office of the farmer and the planter is to produce rather than to destroy; whatever they destroy is to the end that they may produce more abundantly; these persons are therefore natural care-takers. If to this office we add the habit of good housekeeping, we shall have more than one-third of our population at once directly partaking in keeping the earth. It is one of the bitter ironies that farmers should ever have been taken out of their place to wreak vengeance on the earth by means of military devastation. In the past, this ravage has been small in amount because the engines of destruction were weak, but with the perfecting of the modern enginery the havoc is awful and brutal. While we have to our credit the improvement of agriculture and other agencies of conservation, it is yet a fact that man has never been so destructive as now. He is able to turn the skill of his discovery to destructive ends (a subject that we have already approached from another point of view). The keeping of the earth is therefore involved in the organization of society. Military power heads toward destructiveness. Civil power heads toward conservation. The military power may be constructive in times of peace, but its end, if it uses the tools it invents, is devastation and the inflicting of injury. When the civil power is subjugated to the military power, society is headed toward calamity.

To keep and to waste are opposite processes. Not only are we able to despoil the earth by sheer lust of ravage and by blighting the fields with caverns of human slaughter, but we shoot away incredible supplies of copper and petroleum and other unrenewable materials that by every right and equity belong to our successors; and, moreover, we are to make these successors pay for the destruction of their heritage. Day by day we are mortgaging the future, depriving it of supplies that it may need, burdening the shoulders of generations yet unborn.

Merely to make the earth productive and to keep it clean and to bear a reverent regard for its products, is the special prerogative of a good agriculture and a good citizenry founded thereon; this may seem at the moment to be small and ineffective as against mad impersonal and limitless havoc, but it carries the final healing; and while the land worker will bear much of the burden on his back he will also redeem the earth.

The tones of industry

One of the clearest notes of our time is the recognition of the holiness of industry and the attempt to formulate the morals of it. We accept this fact indirectly by the modern endeavor to give the laboring man his due.

The handworker is more or less elemental, dealing directly with the materials. We begin to recognize these industries in literature, in sculpture, and in painting; but we do not yet very consciously or effectively translate them into music.

It is to be recognized, of course, that melody is emotional and dynamic not imitative, that its power lies in suggestion rather than in direct representation, and that its language is general; with all this I have nothing to do. Meunier has done much with his chisel to interpret the spirit of constructive labor and to develop its higher significance. His art is indeed concrete and static, and sculpture and music are not to be compared; yet it raises the question whether there may be other bold extensions of art.

The primitive industries must have been mostly silent, when there were no iron tools, when fire felled the forest tree and hollowed the canoe, when the parts in construction were secured by thongs, and when the game was caught in silent traps or by the swift noiseless arrow and spear. Even at the Stone Age the rude implements and the materials must have been mostly devoid of resonance. But now industry has become universal and complex, and it has also become noisy, —so noisy that we organize to protect ourselves from becoming distraught.

And yet a workshop, particularly if it works in metal, is replete with tones that are essentially musical. Workmen respond readily to unison. There are melodies that arise from

The Tones of Industry

certain kinds of labor. Much of our labor is rhythmic. In any factory driven by power, there is a fundamental rhythm and motion, tying all things together. I have often thought, standing at the threshold of a mill, that it might be possible somewhere by careful forethought to eliminate the clatter and so to organize the work as to develop a better expression in labor. Very much do we need to make industry vocal.

It is worth considering, also, whether it is possible to take over into music any of these sounds of industry in a new way, that they may be given meanings they do not now possess.

At all events, the poetic element in industry is capable of great development and of progressive interpretation; and poetry is scarcely to be dissociated from sound. All good work well done is essentially poetic to the sensitive mind; and when the work is the rhythm of many men acting in unison, the poetry has voice.

> The striking of the rivet
> The purr of a drill
> The crash of a steam-shovel
> The plunge of a dredge
> The buzz of a saw
> The roll of belts and chains
> The whirl of spindles
> The hiss of steam
> The tip-tap of valves
> The undertone rumble of a mill
> The silence intent of men at work
> The talk of men going to their homes,—
> These are all the notes of great symphonies.

Nor should I stop with the industries of commerce and manufacture. There are many possibilities in the sounds and voices that are known of fisherfolk and campers and foresters and farmers. Somehow we should be able to individualize these voices and to give them an artistic expression in some kind of human composition. There are rich suggestions in the voices of the farmyard, the calls of wild creatures, the tones of farm implements and machinery, the sounds of the elements, and particularly in the relations of all these to the pauses, the silences, and the distances beyond.

Whether it is possible to utilize any of these tones and voices artistically is not for a layman to say; but the layman may express the need that he feels.

The threatened literature

A fear seems to be abroad that the inquisitiveness and exactness of science will deprive literature of imagination and sympathy and will destroy artistic expression; and it is said that we are in danger of losing the devotional element in literature. If these apprehensions are well founded, then do we have cause for alarm, seeing that literature is an immeasurable resource.

Great literature may be relatively independent of time and place, and this is beyond discussion here; but if the standards of interpretative literature are lowering it must be because the standards of life are lowering, for the attainment and the outlook of a people are bound to be displayed in its letters.

Perhaps our difficulty lies in a change in methods and standards rather than in essential qualities. We constantly acquire new material for literary use. The riches of life are vaster and deeper than ever before. It would be strange indeed if the new experience of the planet did not express itself in new literary form.

We are led astray by the fatal habit of making comparisons, contrasting one epoch with another. There may be inflexible souls among the investigators who see little or nothing beyond the set of facts in a little field, but surely the greater number of scientific men are persons of keen imagination and of broad interest in all conquests. Indeed, a lively imagination is indispensable in persons of the best attainments in science; it is necessary only that the imagination be regulated and trained. Never has it been so true that fact is stranger than fiction. Never have the flights of the poets been so evenly matched by the flights of science. All great engineers, chemists, physiologists, physicists work in the realm of imagination, of imagination that projects the unknown from the known. Almost do we think that the Roentgen ray, the wireless telegraphy, the analysis of the light of the stars, the serum control of disease are the product of what we might call pure fancy. The very utilities and conquests of modern society are the results of better imagination than the world has yet known. If it is true that the desire to measure and to analyze is now an established trait, equally is it true that it directs the mind into far and untried reaches; and if we have not yet found this range of inspiration in what is called artistic literature, it must be because literary criticism has not accepted the imagery of the modern world and is still looking for its art to the models of the past.

The models of the past are properly the standards for the performances of their time, but this does not constitute them the standards of all time or of the present time. Perhaps the writing of language for the sake of writing it is losing its hold; but a new, clear, and forceful literature appears. This new literature has its own criteria. It would be violence to judge it only by standards of criticism founded on Elizabethan writings. We do not descend into crude materialism because we describe the materials of the cosmos; we do not eliminate imagination because we desire that it shall have meaning; we do not strip literature of artistic quality because it is true to the facts and the outlook of our own time.

It may be admitted that present literature is inadequate, and that we are still obliged to go to the former compositions for our highest artistic expressions. Very good. Let us hope that we shall never cease to want these older literatures. Let us hope that we shall never be severed from our past. But perhaps the good judge in a coming generation, when the slow process of elimination has perfected its criticism, will discover something very noble and even very artistic in the abundant writing of our day. Certainly he will note the recovery from the first excess of reaction against the older orders, and he will be aware that at this epoch man began anew to express his social sense in a large way, as a result of all his painstaking studies in science. Even if he should not discover the highest forms of literary expression, he might find that here was the large promise of a new order. Possibly he would discover major compositions of the excellence of which we ourselves are not aware.

It is less than forty years since Darwin and less than fifty years since Agassiz. It is only twenty years since Pasteur. It is only a century and a quarter since Franklin, fifty years since Faraday, less than twenty-five since Tyndall. It is sixty years since Humboldt glorified the earth with the range of his imagination. It is not so very far even if we go back to Newton and to Kepler. Within the span of a century we count name after name of prophets who have set us on a new course. So complete has been the revolution that we lost our old bearings before we had found the new. We have not yet worked out the new relationships, nor put into practice their moral obligations, nor have we grasped the fulness of our privileges. We have not yet made the new knowledge consciously into a philosophy of life or incorporated it completely into working attitudes of social equity. Therefore, not even now are we ripe for the new literature.

We have gone far enough, however, to know that science is not unsympathetic and that it is not contemptuous of the unknown. By lens and prism and balance and line we measure minutely whatever we can sense; then with bared heads we look out to the great unknown and we cast our lines beyond the stars. There are no realms beyond which the prophecy of science would not go. It resolves the atom and it weighs the planets.

Among the science men I have found as many poetic souls as among the literary men, although they may not know so much poetry, and they are not equally trained in literary expression; being free of the restraint of conventional criticism, they are likely to have a peculiarly keen and sympathetic projection. Close dissection long continued may not lead to free artistic literary expression; this is as true of literary anatomy as of biological anatomy: but this does not destroy the freedom of other souls, and it may afford good material for the artist.

Two kinds of popular writing are confused in the public mind, for there are two classes that express the findings of scientific inquiry. The prevailing product is that which issues from establishments and institutions. This is supervised, edited, and made to conform; it is the product of our perfected organizations and has all the hardness of its origin. The other literature is of a different breed. It is the expression of personality. The one is a useful and necessary public literature of record and advice; the other is a literature of outlook and inspiration. The latter is not to be expected from the institutions, for it is naturally the literature of freedom.

My reader now knows my line of approach to the charge that literature is in danger of losing its element of devotion, and hereby lies the main reason for introducing this discussion into my little book. We may be losing the old literary piety and the technical theology, because we are losing the old theocratic outlook on creation. We also know that the final control of human welfare will not be governmental or military, and we shall some day learn that it will not be economic as we now prevailingly use the word. We have long since forgotten that once it was patriarchal. We shall know the creator in the creation. We shall derive more of our solaces from the creation and in the consciousness of our right relations to it. We shall be more fully aware that righteousness inheres in honest occupation. We shall find some bold and free way in which the human spirit may express itself.

The separate soul

Many times in this journey have we come against the importance of the individual. We are to develop the man's social feeling at the same time that we allow him to remain separate. We are to accomplish certain social results otherwise than by the process of thronging, which is so much a part of the philosophy of this anxious epoch; and therefore we may pursue the subject still a little further.

Any close and worth-while contact with the earth tends to make one original or at least detached in one's judgments and independent of group control. In proportion as society becomes organized and involved, do we need the separate spirit and persons who are responsible beings on their own account. The independent judgment should be much furthered by studies in the sciences that are founded on observation of native forms and conditions. And yet the gains of scientific study become so rigidly organized into great enterprises that the individual is likely to be lost in them.

As an example of what I mean, I mention John Muir, who has recently passed away, and who stood for a definite contribution to his generation. He could hardly have made this contribution if he had been attached to any of the great institutions or organizations or to big business. He has left a personal impression and a remarkable literature that has been very little influenced by group psychology. He is the interpreter of mountains, forests, and glaciers.

There is one method of aggregation and social intercourse. There is another method of isolation and separateness. Never in the open country do I see a young man or woman at nightfall going down the highways and the long fields but I think of the character that develops out of the loneliness, in the silence of vast surroundings, projected against the backgrounds, and of the suggestions that must come from these situations as contrasted with those that arise from the babble of the crowds. There is hardiness in such training; there is independence, the taking of one's own risk and no need of the protection of compensation-acts. There is no over-imposed director to fall back on. Physical recuperation is in the situation. As against these fields, much of the habitual golf and tennis and other adventitious means of killing time and of making up deficiencies is almost ludicrous.

Many of our reformers fail because they express only a group psychology and do not have a living personal interpretation. Undoubtedly many persons who might have had a message of their own have lost it and have also lost the opportunity to express it by belonging to too many clubs and by too continuous association with so-called kindred spirits, or by taking too much post-graduate study. It is a great temptation to join many clubs, but if one feels any stir of originality in himself, he should be cautious how he joins.

I may also recall the great example of Agassiz at Penikese. In his last year, broken in health, feeling the message he still had for the people, he opened the school on the little island off the coast of Massachusetts. It was a short school in one summer only, yet it has made an indelible impression on American education. It stimulates one to know that the person who met the incoming students on the wharf was Agassiz himself, not an assistant or an instructor. Out of the great number of applicants, he chose fifty whom he would teach. He wanted to send forth these chosen persons with his message, apostles to carry the methods and the way of approach. (When are we to have the Penikese for the rural backgrounds?)

Sometime there will be many great unattached teachers, who will choose their own pupils because they want them and not merely because the applicants have satisfied certain arbitrary tests. The students may be graduates of colleges or they may be others. They will pursue their work not for credit or for any other reward. We shall yet come back to the masters, and there will be teaching in the market-places.

We are now in the epoch of great organization not only in industrial developments but also in educational and social enterprises, in religious work, and in governmental activities. So completely is the organization proceeding in every direction, and so good is it, that one habitually and properly desires to identify oneself with some form of associated work. Almost in spite of oneself, one is caught up into the plan of things, and becomes part of a social, economic, or educational mechanism. No longer do we seek our educational institutions so much for the purpose of attaching ourselves to a master as to pursue a course of study. No more do we sit at the feet of Gamaliel.

In government, the organization has recently taken the form of mechanism for efficiency. We want government and all kinds of organization to be efficient and effective, but administrative efficiency may easily proceed at the expense of personality. Much of our public organization for efficiency is essentially monarchic in its tendency. It is likely to eliminate the most precious resource in human society, which is the freedom of expression of the competent individual. We are piling organization on organization, one supervising and watching and "investigating" the other. The greater the number of the commissions, investigating committees, and the interlocking groups, the more complex does the whole process become and the more difficult is it for the person to find himself. We can never successfully substitute bookkeeping for men and women. We are more in need of personality than of administrative regularity.

This is not a doctrine of laissez-faire or let-alone. The very conditions of modern society demand strong control and regulation and vigorous organization; but the danger is that we apply the controls uniformly and everywhere and eliminate the free action of the individual, as if control were in itself a merit.

In some way we must protect the person from being submerged in the system. We need always to get back of the group to the individual. The person is the reason for the group, although he is responsible to the group.

It is probably a great advantage to our democracy that our educational institutions are so completely organized, for by that means we are able to educate many more persons and to prepare them for the world with a clear and direct purpose in life. But this is not the whole of the public educational process. Some of the most useful persons cannot express themselves in institutions. This is not the fault of the institutions. In the nature of their character, these persons are separate. For the most part, they do not now have adequate means of self-expression or of contributing themselves to the public welfare.

When we shall have completed the present necessity of consolidation, centralization, and organization, society will begin to be conscious of the separate souls, who in the nature of the case must stand by themselves, and it will make use of them for the public good. Society will endow persons, not on a basis of salary, and enable them thereby to teach in their own way and their own time. This will represent one of the highest types of endowment by government and society.

We begin to approach this time by the support, through semi-public agencies, of persons to accomplish certain results or to undertake special pieces of work, particularly of research; but we have not yet attained the higher aim of endowing individuals to express themselves personally. There are liberated personalities, rare and prophetic, who are consumed only in making a living but who should be given unreservedly to the people: the people are much in need.

Never have we needed the separate soul so much as now.

The element of separateness in society

If it is so important that we have these separate souls, then must we inquire where they may be found and particularly how we may insure the requisite supply. Isolated separates appear here and there, in all the ranges of human experiences; these cannot be provided or foretold; but we shall need, in days to come, a group or a large class of persons, who in the nature of their occupation, situation, and training are relatively independent and free. We need more than a limited number of strong outstanding figures who rise to personal leadership. We must have a body of unattached laborers and producers who are in sufficient numbers to influence unexpressed public opinion and who will form a natural corrective as against organization-men, habitual reformers, and extremists.

It is apparent that such a class must own productive property, be able to secure support by working for themselves, and produce supplies that are indispensable to society. Their individual interests must be greater and more insistent than their associative interests. They should be in direct contact with native resources. This characterization describes the farmer, and no other large or important group.

We have considered, on a former page, that we are not to look for the self-acting individuals among the workingmen as a class. They are rapidly partaking in an opposite development. They are controlled by associative interests. Even under a profit-sharing system they are parts in a close concert.

How to strike the balance between the needful individualism and social crystallization is probably the most difficult question before society. Of the great underlying classes of occupations, farming is the only one that presents the individualistic side very strongly. If individualism is to be preserved anywhere, it must be preserved here. The tendency of our present-day discussion is to organize the farmers as other groups or masses are organized. We are in danger here. Assuredly, the farmer needs better resources in association, but it is a nice question how far we should go, and how completely we should try to redirect him. Fortunately, the holding of title to land and the separateness of farm habitations prevent solidification. If, on this individualism and without destroying it, we can develop a co-acting and co-operating activity, we shall undoubtedly be on the line of safety as well as on the line of promise. It would be a pity to organize the farming people merely to secure them their "rights." We ought soon to pass this epoch in civilization. There are no "rights" exclusive to any class. "Rights" are not possessions. I do not know where the element of separateness in society is to be derived unless it comes out of the earth.

Given sufficient organization to enable the farmer to express himself fully in his occupation and to secure protection, then we may well let the matter rest until his place in society develops by the operation of natural forces. We cannot allow the fundamental supplies from the common earth to be controlled by arbitrary class regulation. It would be a misfortune if the farmer were to isolate himself by making "demands" on society. I hope that the farmer's obligation may be so sensitively developed in him as to produce a better kind of mass-cohesion than we have yet known.

The democratic basis in agriculture

All these positions are capable of direct application in the incorporation of agriculture into a scheme of democracy. A brief treatment of this subject I had developed for the present book; and this treatment, with applications to particular situations now confronting us, I used recently in the vice-presidential address before the new Section M of the American Association for the Advancement of Science (published in *Science,* February 26, 1915, where the remainder of it may be found). Some of the general points of view, modified from that address, may be brought together here. The desirability of keeping a free and unattached attitude in the people on the land may be expounded in many directions, but for my purpose I will confine the illustrations to organization in the field of education.

The agricultural situation is now much in the public mind. It is widely discussed in the press, which shows that it has news value. Much of this value is merely of superficial and temporary interest. Much of it represents a desire to try new remedies for old ills. Many of these remedies will not work. We must be prepared for some loss of public interest in them as time goes on. We are now in a publicity stage of our rural development. It would seem that the news-gathering and some other agencies discover these movements after the work of many constructive spirits has set them going and has laid real foundations; and not these foundations, but only detached items of passing interest, may be known of any large part of the public. I hope that we shall not be disturbed by this circumstance nor let it interfere with good work or with fundamental considerations, however much we may deplore the false expectations that may result.

The Holy Earth

We are at the parting of the ways. For years without number—for years that run into the centuries when men have slaughtered each other on many fields, thinking that they were on the fields of honor, when many awful despotisms have ground men into the dust, the despotisms thinking themselves divine—for all these years there have been men on the land wishing to see the light, trying to make mankind hear, hoping but never realizing. They have been the pawns on the great battlefields, men taken out of the peasantries to be hurled against other men they did not know and for no rewards except further enslavement. They may even have been developed to a high degree of manual or technical skill that they might the better support governments to make conquests. They have been on the bottom, upholding the whole superstructure and pressed into the earth by the weight of it. When the final history is written, the lot of the man on the land will be the saddest chapter.

But in the nineteenth century, the man at the bottom began really to be recognized politically. This recognition is of two kinds,—the use that a government can make in its own interest of a highly efficient husbandry, and the desire to give the husbandman full opportunity and full justice. I hope that in these times the latter motive always prevails. It is the only course of safety.

Great public-service institutions have now been founded in the rural movement. The United States Department of Agriculture has grown to be one of the notable governmental establishments of the world, extending itself to a multitude of interests and operating with remarkable effectiveness. The chain of colleges of agriculture and experiment stations, generously co-operative between nation and State, is unlike any other development anywhere, meaning more, I think, for the future welfare and peace of the people than any one of us yet foresees. There is the finest fraternalism, and yet without clannishness, between these great agencies, setting a good example in public service. And to these agencies we are to add the State departments of agriculture, the work of private endowments although yet in its infancy, the growing and very desirable contact with the rural field of many institutions of learning. All these agencies comprise a distinctly modern phase of public activity.

A new agency has been created in the agricultural extension act which was signed by President Wilson on the 8th of May in 1914. The farmer is to find help at his own door. A new instrumentality in the world has now received the sanction of a whole people and we are just beginning to organize it. The organization must be extensive, and it ought also to be liberal. No such national plan on such a scale has ever been attempted; and it almost staggers one when one even partly comprehends the tremendous consequences that in all likelihood will come of it. The significance of it is not yet grasped by the great body of the people.

Now, the problem is to relate all this public work to the development of a democracy. I am not thinking so much of the development of a form of government as of a real democratic expression on the part of the people. Agriculture is our basic industry. As we organize its affairs, so to a great degree shall we secure the results in society in general. It is very important in our great experiment in democracy that we do not lose sight of the first principle in democracy, which is to let the control of policies and affairs rest directly back on the people.

We have developed the institutions on public funds to train the farmer and to give him voice. These institutions are of vast importance in the founding of a people. The folk are to be developed in themselves rather than by class legislation, or by favor of government, or by any attitude of benevolence from without.

Whether there is any danger in the organization of our new nationalized extension work, and the other public rural agencies, I suppose not one of us knows. But for myself, I have apprehension of the tendency to make some of the agricultural work into "projects" at Washington and elsewhere. If we are not careful, we shall not only too much centralize the work, but we shall tie it up in perplexing red-tape, official obstacles, and bookkeeping. The merit of the projects themselves and the intentions of the officers concerned in them are not involved in what I say; I speak only of the tendency of all government to formality and to crystallization, to machine work and to armchair regulations; and even at the risk of a somewhat lower so-called "efficiency," I should prefer for such work as investigating and teaching in agriculture, a dispersion of the initiative and responsibility, letting the co-ordination and standardizing arise very much from conference and very little from arbitrary regulation.

The best project anywhere is a good man or woman working in a program, but unhampered.

If it is important that the administration of agricultural work be not overmuch centralized at Washington, it is equally true that it should not be too much centralized in the States. I hear that persons who object strongly to federal concentration may nevertheless decline to give the counties and the communities in their own States the benefit of any useful starting-power and autonomy. In fact, I am inclined to think that here at present lies one of our greatest dangers.

A strong centralization within the State may be the most hurtful kind of concentration, for it may more vitally affect the people at home. Here the question, remember, is not the most efficient formal administration, but the best results for the people. The farm-bureau work, for example, can never produce the background results of which it is capable if it is a strongly intrenched movement pushed out from one centre, as from the college of agriculture or other institution. The college may be the guiding force, but it should not remove responsibility from the people of the localities, or offer them a kind of co-operation that is only the privilege of partaking in the college enterprises. I fear that some of our so-called co-operation in public work of many kinds is little more than to allow the co-operator to approve what the official administration has done.

In the course of our experience in democracy, we have developed many checks against too great centralization. I hope that we may develop the checks effectively in this new welfare work in agriculture, a desire that I am aware is also strong with many of those who are concerned in the planning of it.

Some enterprises may be much centralized, whether in a democracy or elsewhere; an example is the postal service: this is on the business side of government. Some enterprises should be decentralized; an example is a good part of the agricultural service: this is on the educational side of government. It is the tendency to reduce all public work to uniformity; yet there is no virtue in uniformity. Its only value is as a means to an end.

Thus far, the rural movement has been wholesomely democratic. It has been my privilege for one-third of a century to have known rather closely many of the men and women who have been instrumental in bringing the rural problem to its present stage of advancement. They have been public-minded, able, far-seeing men and women, and they have rendered an unmeasurable service. The rural movement has been brought to its present state without any demand for special privilege, without bolstering by factitious legislation, and to a remarkable degree without self-seeking. It is based on a real regard for the welfare of all the people, rather than for rural people exclusively.

Thrice or more in this book I have spoken as if not convinced that the present insistence on "efficiency" in government is altogether sound. That is exactly the impression I desire to convey. As the term is now commonly applied, it is not a measure of good government.

Certain phrases and certain sets of ideas gain dominance at certain times. Just now the idea of administrative efficiency is uppermost. It seems necessarily to be the controlling factor in the progress of any business or any people. Certainly, a people should be efficient; but an efficient government may not mean an efficient people,—it may mean quite otherwise or even the reverse. The primary purpose of government in these days, and particularly in this country, is to educate and to develop all the people and to lead them to express themselves freely and to the full, and to partake politically. And this is what governments may not do, and this is where they may fail even when their efficiency in administration is exact. A monarchic form may be executively more efficient than a democratic form; a despotic form may be more efficient than either. The justification of a democratic form of government lies in the fact that it is a means of education.

The final test of government is not executive efficiency. Every movement, every circumstance that takes starting-power and incentive away from the people, even though it makes for exacter administration, is to be challenged. It is specially to be deplored if this loss of starting-power affects the persons who deal first-hand with the surface of the planet and with the products that come directly out of it.

There is a broad political significance to all this. Sooner or later the people rebel against intrenched or bureaucratic groups. Many of you know how they resist even strongly centralized departments of public instruction, and how the effectiveness of such departments may be jeopardized and much lessened by the very perfectness of their organization; and if they were to engage in a custom of extraneous forms of newsgiving in the public press, the resentment would be the greater. In our rural work we are in danger of developing a piece of machinery founded on our fundamental industry; and if this ever comes about, we shall find the people organizing to resist it.

The reader will understand that in this discussion I assume the agricultural work to be systematically organized, both in nation and State; this is essential to good effort and to the accomplishing of results: but we must take care that the

The Democratic Basis in Agriculture

formal organization does not get in the way of the good workers, hindering and repressing them and wasting their time.

We want governments to be economical and efficient with funds and in the control of affairs; this also is assumed: but we must not overlook the larger issues. In all this new rural effort, we should maintain the spirit of team-work and of co-action, and not make the mistake of depending too much on the routine of centralized control.

In this country we are much criticized for the cost of government and for the supposed control of affairs by monopoly. The cost is undoubtedly too great, but it is the price we pay for the satisfaction of using democratic forms. As to the other disability, let us consider that society lies between two dangers,—the danger of monopoly and the danger of bureaucracy. On the one side is the control of the necessities of life by commercial organization. On the other side is the control of the necessities of life, and even of life itself, by intrenched groups that ostensibly represent the people and which it may be impossible to dislodge. Here are the Scylla and the Charybdis between which human society must pick its devious way.

Both are evil. Of the two, monopoly may be the lesser: it may be more easily brought under control; it tends to be more progressive; it extends less far; it may be the less hateful. They are only two expressions of one thing, one possibly worse than the other. Probably there are peoples who pride themselves on more or less complete escape from monopoly who are nevertheless suffering from the most deadening bureaucracy.

Agriculture is in the foundation of the political, economic, and social structure. If we cannot develop starting-power in the background people, we cannot maintain it elsewhere. The greatness of all this rural work is to lie in the results and not in the methods that absorb so much of our energy. If agriculture cannot be democratic, then there is no democracy.

The background spaces.—The forest

"This is the forest primeval." These are the significant words of the poet in Evangeline. Perhaps more than any single utterance they have set the American youth against the background of the forest.

The backgrounds are important. The life of every one of us is relative. We miss our destiny when we miss or forget our backgrounds. We lose ourselves. Men go off in vague heresies when they forget the conditions against which they live. Judgments become too refined and men tend to become merely disputatious and subtle.

The backgrounds are the great unoccupied spaces. They are the large environments in which we live but which we do not make. The backgrounds are the sky with its limitless reaches; the silences of the sea; the tundra in pallid arctic nights; the deserts with their prismatic colors; the shores that gird the planet; the vast mountains that are beyond reach; the winds, which are the universal voice in nature; the sacredness of the night; the elemental simplicity of the open fields; and the solitude of the forest. These are the facts and situations that stand at our backs, to which we adjust our civilization, and by which we measure ourselves.

The great conquest of mankind is the conquest of his natural conditions. We admire the man who overcomes: the sailor or navigator in hostile and unknown seas; the engineer who projects himself hard against the obstacles; the miner and the explorer; the builder; the farmer who ameliorates the earth to man's use.

But even though we conquer or modify the physical conditions against which we are set, nevertheless the backgrounds will remain. I hope that we may always say "The forest primeval." I hope that some reaches of the sea may never be sailed, that some swamps may never be drained, that some mountain peaks may never be scaled, that some forests may never be harvested. I hope that some knowledge may never be revealed.

Look at your map of the globe. Note how few are the areas of great congestion of population and of much human activity as compared with the vast and apparently empty spaces. How small are the spots that represent the cities and what a little part of the earth are the political divisions that are most in the minds of men! We are likely to think that all these outlying and thinly peopled places are the wastes. I suspect that they contribute more to the race than we think. I am glad that there are still some places of mystery, some reaches of hope, some things far beyond us, some spaces to conjure up dreams. I am glad that the earth is not all Iowa or Belgium or the Channel Islands. I am glad that some of it is the hard hills of New England, some the heathered heights of Scotland, some the cold distances of Quebec, some of it the islands far off in little-traversed seas, and some of it also the unexplored domains that lie within eyesight of our own homes. It is well to know that these spaces exist, that there are places of escape. They add much to the ambition of the race; they make for strength, for courage, and for renewal.

In the cities I am always interested in the variety of the contents of the store windows. Variously fabricated and disguised, these materials come from the ends of the earth. They come from the shores of the seas, from the mines, from the land, from the forests, from the arctic, and from the tropic. They are from the backgrounds. The cities are great, but how much greater are the forests and the sea!

No people should be forbidden the influence of the forest. No child should grow up without a knowledge of the forest; and I mean a real forest and not a grove or village trees or a park. There are no forests in cities, however many trees there may be. As a city is much more than a collection of houses, so is a forest much more than a collection of trees. The forest has its own round of life, its characteristic attributes, its climate, and its inhabitants. When you enter a real forest you enter the solitudes, you are in the unexpressed distances. You walk on the mould of years and perhaps of ages. There is no other wind like the wind of the forest; there is no odor like the odor of the forest; there is no solitude more complete; there is no song of a brook like the song of a forest brook; there is no call of a bird like that of a forest bird; there are no mysteries so deep and which seem yet to be within one's realization.

While a forest is more than trees, yet the trees are the essential part of the forest; and no one ever really knows or understands a forest until he first understands a tree. There is no thing in nature finer and stronger than the bark of a tree; it is a thing in place, adapted to its ends, perfect in its conformation, beautiful in its color and its form and the sweep of its contour; and every bark is peculiar to its species. I think that one never really likes a tree until he is impelled to embrace it with his arms and to run his fingers through the grooves of its bark.

Man listens in the forest. He pauses in the forest. He finds himself. He loses himself in the town and even perhaps in the university. He may lose himself in business and in great affairs; but in the forest he is one with a tree, he stands by himself and yet has consolation, and he comes back to his own place in the scheme of things. We have almost forgotten to listen; so great and ceaseless is the racket that the little voices pass over our ears and we hear them not. I have asked person after person if he knew the song of the chipping-sparrow, and most of them are unaware that it has any song. We do not hear it in the blare of the city street, in railway travel, or when we are in a thunderous crowd. We hear it in the still places and when our ears are ready to catch the smaller sounds. There is no music like the music of the forest, and the better part of it is faint and far away or high in the tops of trees.

The Background Spaces

The forest may be an asylum. "The groves were God's first temples." We need all our altars and more, but we need also the sanctuary of the forest. It is a poor people that has no forests. I prize the farms because they have forests. It is a poor political philosophy that has no forests. It is a poor nation that has no forests and no workers in wood.

In many places there are the forests. I think that we do not get the most out of them. Certainly they have two uses: one for the products, and one for the human relief and the inspiration. I should like to see a movement looking toward the better utilization of the forests humanly, as we use school buildings and church buildings and public halls. I wish that we might take our friends to the forests as we also take them to see the works of the masters. For this purpose, we should not go in large companies. We need sympathetic guidance. Parties of two and four may go separately to the forests to walk and to sit and to be silent. I would not forget the forest in the night, in the silence and the simplicity of the darkness. Strangely few are the people who know a real forest at dark. Few are those who know the forest when the rain is falling or when the snow covers the earth. Yet the forest is as real in all these moments as when the sun is at full and the weather is fair.

I wish that we might know the forest intimately and sensitively as a part of our background. I think it would do much to keep us close to the verities and the essentials.

A forest background for a reformatory

Some years ago I presented to a board that was charged with establishing and maintaining a new State reformatory for wayward and delinquent boys an outline of a possible setting for the enterprise; and as this statement really constitutes a practical application of some of the foregoing discussions, I present the larger part of it here. With delinquents it is specially important to develop the sense of obligation and responsibility, and I fear that we are endeavoring to stimulate this sense too exclusively by means of direct governing and disciplinary methods. The statement follows.

I think that the activities in the proposed reformatory should be largely agricultural and industrial. So far as possible the young men should be put into direct contact with realities and with useful and practical work. An effort should be made to have all this work mean something to them and not to be merely make-believe. It is fairly possible to develop such a property and organization as will put them in touch with real work rather than to force the necessity of setting tasks in order to keep them busy.

Aside from the manual labor part of it, the background of the reformatory should be such as will develop the feeling of responsibility in the workers. This means that they must come actually in contact with the raw materials and with things as they grow. When a young man has a piece of wood or metal given to him in a shop, his whole responsibility is merely to make something out of this material; he has no responsibility for the material itself, as he would have if he had been obliged to mine it or to grow it. One of the greatest advantages of a farm training is that it develops a man's responsibility toward the materials with which he works. He is always brought face to face with the problem of saving the fertility of the land, saving the crops, saving the forests, and saving the livestock. The idea of saving and safeguarding these materials is only incidental to those who do not help to produce them.

It is important that the farm of this reformatory should be large enough so that all the young men may do some real pieces of work on it. Such a farm is not to be commercial in the ordinary farming sense. Its primary purpose is to aid in a reformative or educational process. You should, therefore, undertake such types of farming as will best serve those needs and best meet the abilities of the inmates. A very highly specialized farming, as the growing of truck-crops, would be quite impracticable as a commercial enterprise because this kind of farming demands the greatest skill and also because it requires a property very easily accessible to our great markets and, therefore, very expensive to procure and difficult to find in large enough acreage for an institution of this size; and it is doubtful whether this type of farming would have the best effect on the inmates. Of course, I should expect that the institution would try to grow its own vegetables, but it would probably be unwise to make truck-gardening the backbone of the farming enterprise. I also feel that it would not be best to make it primarily a dairy farm or a fruit farm or a poultry farm, although all these things should be well represented on the place and in sufficient extent to supply the institution in whole or in part.

There should be such a farming enterprise as would give a very large and open background, part of it practically wild, and which would allow for considerable freedom of action on the part of the inmates. You should have operations perhaps somewhat in the rough and which would appeal to the manly qualities of the young men. It seems to me that a forestry enterprise would possibly be the best as the main part of the farming scheme.

If the reformatory could have one thousand acres of forest, the area would provide a great variety of conditions that the inmates would have to meet, it would give work in the building of roads and culverts and trails, it would provide winter activity at a time when the other farming enterprises are slack, it would bring the inmates directly in touch with wild and native life, and it would also place them against the natural resources in such a way as to make them feel their responsibility for the objects and the supplies.

Perhaps it will be impossible to secure one thousand acres of good timber in a more or less continuous area. However, it might be possible to assemble a good number of contiguous farms in some of the hill regions so that one thousand acres of timber in various grades of maturity might be secured. There would be open spaces which ought to be planted, and this of itself would provide good work and supervision. The trimming, felling, and other care of this forest would be continuous. The forest should not be stripped, but merely the merchantable or ready timber removed from year to year, and the domain kept in a growing and recuperating condition. One thousand acres of forest, in which timber is fit to be cut, should produce an annual increase of two hundred thousand to three hundred thousand board feet, and this increase should not lessen as the years go on. This timber should be manufactured. I have not looked into the question as to whether a market could be found for the materials that would be made from this timber, but I should suppose that a market could be as readily secured for this kind of manufacture as for any other. The educational and moral effect of seeing the material grow, then caring for it, then harvesting it, and then manufacturing it would be very great. One could follow the process from beginning to end and feel a responsibility for it in every stage. I should suppose that the manufacture would be of small work and not merely the sawing of lumber. It might be well to determine whether there would be market for chairs, cabinets, and other furniture, whip-stocks, or small material that could be used in the manufacture of novelties and other like articles. Possibly the reformatory could supply some of the stock to the prisons that are manufacturing furniture, although the educational and moral effects would be better if the inmates could see the process from beginning to end.

Of course, you would not limit the manufacturing activities of the reformatory to wood-working. You probably would be obliged to have other kinds of factories, but the wood-working shops ought to be part of the plan and I should hope a very important part.

I have not made any careful study of this question, and do not know how feasible these suggestions may be; but they appeal to me very strongly on the educational and reformational end. These suggestions are made only that they may be considered along with other suggestions, and if they seem to be worth while, to have the question investigated.

If something like one thousand acres of land were secured for a forest, it would mean that the farm itself would be rather large. There ought to be probably not less than two or three hundred acres of land that might be used for grazing, gardens, and the ordinary farm operations that would contribute to the support of the inmates of the institution. Of course, this arable land ought to be valley land or at least fairly level and accessible along good public highways. The forest land could be more remote, running back on the hills. If the property could be so located that the forest would control the sources of important streams and springs, the results would be all the better. The young men should feel their responsibility for creeks and ponds, and for the protection of wild life as well as for the crops that they raise.

Where the reformatory should be located is a matter that should receive very careful attention. It is not alone the problem of finding a site that is proper for a reformatory, but also the question of so placing it that it will have some relation to State development and some connection with the people's interests and desires. State institutions should be so separated that the greatest number of people may see them or come into contact with them. I dislike the tendency to group the State institutions about certain populous centres. In these days of easy transportation, the carrying problem is really of less importance than certain less definite but none the less real relations to all the people. There are certain great areas in the State of considerable population in which there are no State institutions, and in which the people know nothing about such affairs beyond the local school and church. Perhaps at first blush the people of a locality might not relish the idea of having a reformatory in their midst, but this feeling ought soon to pass away; and, moreover, the people should be made to feel their responsibility for reformatories, asylums, and penitentiaries as well as their responsibility for any other State institutions, and the feeling should not be encouraged that such institutions should be put somewhere else merely because one locality does not desire them.

The character of the property that is purchased will determine to a very large extent the character of the institution, and, therefore, the nature of the reformatory processes. This is more important than transportation facilities. It is a more important question even than that of the proper buildings, for buildings for these purposes have been studied by many experts and our ideas concerning them have been more or less standardized and, moreover, buildings can be extended and modified more easily than can the landed area. It seems to me that before you think actually of purchasing the land, you should arrive at a fairly definite conclusion as to what kind of a farming enterprise it is desired to develop as a background for the institution; you could then determine as far as possible on principle in what general region the institution ought to be located; and then set out on a direct exploration to determine whether the proper kind and quantity of land can be secured.

The background spaces.—The open fields

Here not long ago was the forest primeval. Here the trees sprouted, and grew their centuries, and returned to the earth. Here the midsummer brook ran all day long from the far-away places. Here the night-winds slept. Here havened the beasts and fowls when storms pursued them. Here the leaves fell in the glory of the autumn, here other leaves burst forth in the miracle of spring, and here the pewee called in the summer. Here the Indian tracked his game.

It was not so very long ago. That old man's father remembers it. Then it was a new and holy land, seemingly fresh from the hand of the creator. The old man speaks of it as of a golden time, now far away and hallowed; he speaks of it with an attitude of reverence. "Ah yes," my father told me; and calmly with bared head he relates it, every incident so sacred that not one hairbreadth must he deviate. The church and the master's school and the forest,—these three are strong in his memory.

Yet these are not all. He remembers the homes cut in the dim wall of the forest. He recalls the farms full of stumps and heaps of logs and the ox-teams on them, for these were in his boyhood. The ox-team was a natural part of the slow-moving conquest in those rugged days. Roads betook themselves into the forest, like great serpents devouring as they went. And one day, behold! the forest was gone. Farm joined farm, the village grew, the old folk fell away, new people came whose names had to be asked.

And I thought me why these fields are not as hallowed as were the old forests. Here are the same knolls and hills. In this turf there may be still the fibres of ancient trees. Here are the paths of the midsummer brooks, but vocal now only in the freshets. Here are the winds. The autumn goes and the spring comes. The pewee calls in the groves. The farmer and not the Indian tracks the plow.

Here I look down on a little city. There is a great school in it. There are spires piercing the trees. In the distance are mills, and I see the smoke of good accomplishment roll out over the hillside. It is a self-centred city, full of pride. Every mile-post praises it. Toward it all the roads lead. It tells itself to all the surrounding country. And yet I cannot but feel that these quiet fields and others like them have made this city; but I am glad that the fields are not proud.

One day a boy and one day a girl will go down from these fields, and out into the thoroughways of life. They will go far, but these hills they will still call home.

From these uplands the waters flow down into the streams that move the mills and that float the ships. Loads of timber still go hence for the construction down below. Here go building-stones and sand and gravel,—gravel from the glaciers. Here goes the hay for ten thousand horses. Here go the wheat, and here the apples, and the animals. Here are the votes that hold the people steady.

Somewhere there is the background. Here is the background. Here things move slowly. Trees grow slowly. The streams change little from year to year, and yet they shape the surface of the earth in this hill country. In yonder fence-row the catbird has built since I was a boy, and yet I have wandered far and I have seen great changes in yonder city. The well-sweep has gone but the well is still there: the wells are gone from the city. The cows have changed in color, but still they are cows and yield their milk in season. The fields do not perish, but time eats away the city. I think all these things must be good and very good or they could not have persisted in all this change.

In the beginning! Yes, I know, it was holy then. The forces of eons shaped it: still was it holy. The forest came: still holy. Then came the open fields.

The background spaces.—The ancestral sea

The planet is not all land, and the sea is as holy as the soil. We speak of the "waste of waters," and we still offer prayers for those who go down to the sea in ships.

Superstition yet clings about the sea. The landsman thinks of the sea as barren, and he regrets that it is not solid land on which he may grow grass and cattle. And as one looks over the surface of the waters, with no visible object on the vast expanse and even the clouds lying apparently dead and sterile, and when one considers that three-fourths of the earth's surface is similarly covered, one has the impression of utter waste and desolation, with no good thing abiding there for the comfort and cheer of man.

The real inhabitants of the sea are beneath the surface and every part is tenanted, so completely tenanted that the ocean produces greater bulk of life, area for area, than does the solid land; and every atom of this life is as keen to live and follows as completely the law of its existence as does the life of the interiors of the continents. The vast meadows of plankton and nekton, albeit largely of organisms microscopic, form a layer for hundreds of feet beneath the surface and on which the great herbivora feed; and on these animals the legions of the carnivora subsist. Every vertical region has its life, peculiar to it, extending even to the bottoms of the depths in the world-slimes and the darkness; and in these deeps the falling remains of the upper realms, like gentle primeval rains, afford a never-failing, never-ending source of food and maintain the slow life in the bottoms. We think of the huge animals of the sea when we think of mass, and it is true that the great whales are the bulkiest creatures we know to have lived; yet it is the bacteria, the desmids, the minute crustaceans, and many other diminutive forms that everywhere populate the sea from the equator to the poles and provide the vast background of the ocean life. In these gulfs of moving unseen forms nitrification proceeds, and the rounds of life go on unceasingly. The leviathan whale strains out these minute organisms from the volumes of waters, and so full of them may be his maw that his captors remove the accumulation with spades. The rivers bring down their freight of mud and organic matter, and supply food for the denizens of the sea. The last remains of all these multitudes are laid down on the ocean floors as organic oozes; and nobody knows what part the abysmal soil may play in the economy of the plant in some future epoch.

The rains of the land come from the sea; the clouds come ultimately from the sea; the trade-winds flow regularly from the sea; the temperatures of the land surface are controlled largely from the sea; the high lands are washed into the sea as into a basin; if all the continents were levelled into the sea still would the sea envelop the planet about two miles deep. Impurities find their way into the sea and are there digested into the universal beneficence. We must reckon with the sea.

It is supposed that the first life on the earth came forth where the land and the waters join, from that eternal interplay of cosmic forces where the solid and the fluid, the mobile and the immobile, meet and marry.

Verily, the ancestral sea is the background of the planet. Its very vastness makes it significant. It shows no age. Its deeps have no doubt existed from the solidification of the earth and they will probably remain when all works of man perish utterly.

The sea is the bosom of the earth's mysteries. Because man cannot set foot on it, the sea remains beyond his power to modify, to handle, and to control. No breach that man may make but will immediately fill; no fleets of mighty ships go down but that the sea covers them in silence and knows them not; man may not hold converse with the monsters in the deeps. The sea is beyond him, surpassing, elemental, and yet blessing him with abundant benedictions.

So vast is the sea and so self-recuperating that man cannot sterilize it. He despoils none of its surface when he sails his ships. He does not annihilate the realms of plankton, lying layer on layer in its deluging, consuming soil. It controls him mightily.

The seas and the shores have provided the trading ways of the peoples. The ocean connects all lands, surrounds all lands. Until recent times the great marts have been mostly on coasts or within easy water access of them. The polity of early settlements was largely the polity of the sea and the strand. The daring of the navigator was one of the first of the heroic human qualities. Probably all dry land was once under the sea, and therefrom has it drawn much of its power.

From earliest times the sea has yielded property common to all and free to whomever would take it,—the fish, the wrack, the drift, the salvage of ships. Pirates have roamed the sea for spoil and booty. When government appropriates the wreckage of ships and the stranded derelict of the sea, the people may think it justifiable protection of their rights to secrete it. Smuggling is an old sea license. Laws and customs and old restraints lose their force and vanish on the sea; and freedom rises out of the sea.

And so the ocean has contributed to the making of the outlook of the human family. The race would be a very different race had there been no sea stretching to the unknown, conjuring vague fears and stimulating hopes, bringing its freight, bearing tidings of far lands, sundering traditions, rolling the waves of its elemental music, driving its rank smells into the nostrils, putting its salt into the soul.

Chronology
The Life of Liberty Hyde Bailey

March 15, 1858: Liberty Hyde Bailey is born in South Haven, Michigan, the son of pioneer parents who had cleared the wilderness and established a farm near the shores of Lake Michigan.

1877–1882: Bailey studies at the State Agricultural College, (now known as Michigan State University) and studies with Professor William James Beal, a botanist who emphasizes direct observation and experiments with plants as a supplement to textbooks.

1883–1884: Bailey attends Harvard University as an assistant to Professor Asa Gray. It is at this time he develops his abilities in taxonomic classification.

1885: Bailey returns to State as Professor and Chair of Horticulture and Landscape Gardening. Here he establishes the first horticulture department in the United States. While at State, he travels throughout the state speaking at Grange meetings, fairs, and farmers' institutes. He firmly believes in keeping "grassroots" contacts with farm people, and this is a hallmark of his ideas on extension work. During this time Bailey develops a plan for his life, which included twenty-five years for training and learning in his profession, twenty-five years of employment and public service, and twenty-five years in retirement in doing as he pleased.

1888: Bailey designs and builds the first laboratory in the United State devoted to scientific horticulture. The building, now known at Eustace-Cole Hall, still stands and is listed on the National Register

1888: Bailey leaves State and goes to Cornell as Professor of General and Experimental Horticulture. He is an inspiring teacher who frequents the orchards, gardens, and laboratories in the region. His horticultural writings continue, and he clarifies and makes accessible botanical knowledge and applies it to agriculture and horticulture. He realizes a need to give the farmer and scientist a common language. He organizes facts as well as experts from all over the world; the results are the *Cyclopedia of American Horticulture*, the *Standard Cyclopedia of Horticulture*, and *Hortus*. He would eventually author 63 books, co-author 4, edit 117 books and 6 cyclopedias and directories, write more than 1,300 articles, and edit several magazines.

1893: He is a founding member of the Botanical Society of America.

1894: New York State grants the first public funds to Cornell to use in the teaching of nature-study in New York rural schools. Bailey uses the funds for the publication of the *Rural School Leaflets*. These leaflets, distributed to schools across the state, result in the formation of Junior Naturalist Clubs, later called Boys and Girls Clubs, which are the forerunner of today's 4-H Youth Programs. His goal in teaching children was simple and practical: "to open the child's mind by direct observation to a knowledge and love of the common things and experiences in his environment."

1903: Bailey becomes the Dean of the College of Agriculture and is one of the founders and first president of the American Society for Horticultural Science.

1906: Bailey becomes president of the Association of American Agricultural Colleges and Experiment Stations.

1907: The Semicentennial of Michigan Agricultural College (MAC, formerly the State Agricultural College) is held with the meeting of the Association of American Agricultural Colleges and Experiment Stations on the MAC campus. President Theodore Roosevelt is present and asks Bailey to chair the new Commission on Country Life.

1908: President Roosevelt officially appoints Bailey as chair of the Commission on Country Life. The commission's task is to determine why people are leaving their farms for city life and to make recommendations for improvements. After two years works and thousands of meetings and miles traveled he writes the *Report of the Commission on Country Life*. This report is thought to have had more impact than any other document for rural reform.

1908: Bailey founds and becomes the first president of the American Nature Study Society.

1913: Bailey retires from Cornell and continues writing, exploring, and traveling the world to collect plants.

1914: Bailey writes *The Holy Earth* while aboard a ship on the way to New Zealand. The book, which sums up a philosophy he had been developing for years, is written on the backs of letters and on scraps of paper-anything at hand. Though the book is not a financial success, Bailey nevertheless feels it will endure.

1914: The Smith-Lever Act passes a result of the Commission on Country Life's work establishing the Extension Service and 4-H Youth Programs. In addition the commission's work helped launch agricultural education in schools, initiation of the U.S. Parcel Post system, and the beginnings of support for rural electrification and communication systems to rural areas.

1925: Bailey is named president of the International Botanical Congress, where his efforts lead to amending the international rules of nomenclature.

1926: Bailey becomes president of the American Association for the Advancement of Science.

1935–1952: Bailey donates his vast collections of plants to Cornell to establish the Hortorium, a word he invented; a repository of things of the garden, their documentation and classification.

1948: Cornell University celebrates Bailey's 90th birthday. At the event Bailey remarks: "It is a marvelous planet on which we ride. It is a great privilege to live thereon, to partake in the journey, and to experience its goodness. We may co-operate rather than rebel. We should try to find the meanings rather than to be satisfied only with the spectacles. My life has been a continuous fulfillment of dreams."

December 25th, 1954: Liberty Hyde Bailey dies at his home in Ithaca, New York, at 96. He set lofty goals and made tremendous contributions to horticulture bringing horticulture from a craft to a science. During his lifetime he was the recipient of several honorary doctorates and numerous international and national awards.

March 15, 1958: The Postmaster General authorizes a commemorative first class postage stamp honoring Gardening and Horticulture in recognition of the Centennial of Bailey's birth.

JANE L. TAYLOR
Founding Curator Michigan 4-H Children's Garden
Michigan State University

The Liberty Hyde Bailey Museum

THE LIBERTY Hyde Bailey Museum—a National Historic Site in
South Haven, Michigan—is the birthplace of the world renowned
botanist, horticulturist, philosopher, environmentalist, and educational reformer, Dr. Liberty Hyde Bailey. Built in 1856, this
architectural artifact of Michigan's agricultural past includes
personal items of the Bailey family and regional artifacts of the
southwest Michigan fruit belt.

The museum, gifted to the City of South Haven in 1938, is
dedicated to the preservation and collection of items relating
to the life and work of Dr. Liberty Hyde Bailey; significant artifacts and information of the fruit industry in western Michigan;
information dealing with other prominent horticulturalists
and botanists from Bailey's field; items relating to the cultural
and documentary history of the City of South Haven and maintenance of the home and grounds as they might have been in
Dr. Bailey's time. The museum offers programs and events
throughout the year demonstrating the link between botany,
horticulture, agriculture and everyday life.